# FINANCIAL ASTROLOGY

## *Almanac 2026*

*Trading & Investing Using the Planets*

*M.G. Bucholtz, B.Sc, MBA, M.Sc.*

A WOOD DRAGON BOOK

Financial Astrology Almanac 2026

*Trading & Investing Using the Planets*



Published by:
Wood Dragon Books
Box 429, Mossbank, Saskatchewan, Canada, S0H 3G0
http://www.wooddragonbooks.com

ISBN: 978-1-997860-04-4 (Paperback)
ISBN : 978-1-997860-06-8 (eBook)
ISBN: 978-1-997860-05-1 (Hardcover)

Contact the author at: supercyclereport@gmail.com or visit www.investingsuccess.ca

# *DEDICATION*

To the many traders and investors who, at some visceral level, suspect there is more to the financial market system than P/E ratios and analyst recommendations.

Our solar system is a 'resonance machine' held in motion by the axial rotations and the orbital movements of the planets around the Sun. These interwoven, interdependent movements are capable of imparting a gravitational torque force to the surface layers of the Sun. In response, the Sun displays sunspots and emits increased amounts of solar radiation into the vastness of space. The residual radiation that penetrates Earth's geomagnetic field has a profound cyclical influence on not only our weather patterns but also on human emotion; the same emotion that causes us to either buy or sell on the financial markets.

After reading this Almanac, you will view the markets in a completely different way; trading and investing will take on a whole new dimension.

# *DISCLAIMER*

All material provided herein is based on material gleaned from mathematical and astronomical publications researched by the author to supplement his own trading. This publication is written for those who actively trade and invest in the financial markets and who are looking to incorporate astrological phenomena and esoteric math into their market activity. While the material presented herein has proven reliable to the author in his personal trading and investing activity, there is no guarantee this material will continue to be reliable into the future.

The author and publisher assume no liability whatsoever for any investment or trading decisions made by readers of this book. The reader alone is responsible for all trading and investment outcomes and is further advised not to exceed his or her risk tolerances when trading or investing in the financial markets.

# *TABLE OF CONTENTS*

INTRODUCTION

CHAPTER 1: *Fundamentals*

CHAPTER 2: *Fibonacci*

CHAPTER 3: *Planetary Resonance*

CHAPTER 4: *Sunspots*

CHAPTER 5: *Sun and Moon Cycles*

CHAPTER 6: *Mercury Cycles*

CHAPTER 7: *Venus Cycles*

CHAPTER 8: *Earth, Jupiter, and Saturn*

CHAPTER 9: *Equity and Commodity Cycles*

CHAPTER 10: *Longer Cycles*

CHAPTER 11: *George Bayer's Rules*

CHAPTER 12: *2026 in Summary*

FINAL WORDS

NOTES

GLOSSARY

APPENDIX 1

ABOUT THE AUTHOR

OTHER BOOKS BY THE AUTHOR

# INTRODUCTION

Many traders and investors think company press releases, media news opinions, quarterly earnings reports, and analyst targets drive stock prices and major index movements. I disagree.

I believe price action is driven by human emotion. Many psychologists describe six emotions: happy, sad, fear, disgust, anger, and surprise. I have a shorter list. I believe fear and greed are the two classes of emotion that influence the financial markets. When we are greedy, we run towards the market. We buy, buy, buy. When we are fearful, we run away from the market. We sell, sell, sell.

Ancient civilizations as far back as the Sumerians recognized the changeable nature of human emotion. Their high priests correlated emotional changes to movements of Mercury, Venus, Mars, Jupiter, and Saturn in the heavens. They assigned to these planets the names of the various deities revered by the people. They also identified and named various star constellations in the heavens. They then divided the heavens into twelve segments. Each segment was correlated to the most significant star constellation in it. This was the beginning of a fascination with the planets; the birth of *astrology* as we know it today.

The first few decades of the $20^{th}$ century marked a milestone in astrology when people began making connections between the planets and the financial markets. Consider W.D. Gann and George Bayer. In the first few decades of the 1900s, W.D. Gann reportedly made handsome trading profits when he realized that cyclical planetary aspects bore a striking correlation to financial market cyclical price action. Gann is most famous for identifying the Saturn/Jupiter cycle which he labelled the *Gann Master Cycle*. George Bayer was a German immigrant who landed in New York around 1899. He arrived armed with substantial knowledge of the solar system. He reportedly made a comfortable living trading commodity futures using planetary movements. In the late 1930s, he published several books which contained references to his 'Rules'. Many of his rules hold up to scrutiny yet today. And we must not forget about Louise McWhirter. In the mid-1930s, she illuminated a further connection between the stock market and the cosmos when she identified an 18.6-year cyclical correlation to the position of the North Node of the Moon in the zodiac. Her data showed that as the Node entered the sign of Aquarius, the economy and stock market would be making a bottom. In 1937, she published her findings as *The McWhirter Theory of Stock Market Forecasting.*

However, in the late 1940s, correlations between the planets and the financial markets were becoming too well known about by individual investors. The powerful banking interests on Wall Street could not tolerate this reality so they engaged academia to control the narrative. Leading economic thinkers at universities like Yale, Harvard, and Chicago developed *Modern Portfolio Theory* and the *Efficient Market Hypothesis.*

The idea of *Modern Portfolio Theory* was developed by Harry Markowitz who advocated for investors to assemble a diversified portfolio of investments to better control risk. Paul Samuelson laid the groundwork for the *Efficient Market Hypothesis* when he said that prices of stocks reflect all currently available information; earning an investment return greater than that of the overall market is therefore impossible. These works promoted the idea that the markets could not be timed; investing was for the long term and investors should buy, hold, and forget about the interim ups and downs of the market.

The academics were successful. The connection between the planets and the market faded from everyday discourse. These academic ideas persisted for several decades to follow and underpinned the rise of the mutual fund industry and the hedge fund movement. However, these ideas came under severe scrutiny, first with the Long Term Capital debacle in 1998 which required a $3.6 billion government bailout to stave off collapse of the financial system. This shock was followed by the bursting of severely overpriced technology stocks in 2000. Yet another shock came with the 2008 sub-prime mortgage collapse that again required a massive bailout to stave off derailment of the global economy. Today, despite these market meltdowns, neither of these academic ideas has ever been proven; they remain a theory and a hypothesis. Yet, the investment industry continues to cling to them as if they were hard and fast scientific laws.

The failure of these academic ideas to predict these market shocks brought financial astrology to the fore again. Since the 2008 crisis, the application of planetary science to the stock market has been made more user friendly. The software designers at Australian company *Optuma* Pty Ltd. have created an impressive financial astrology platform which they have built into their Optuma software program (which has been used to generate the charts in this Almanac). Software designers at U.S. firm Astrolabe developed *Solar Fire Gold* which generates horoscope wheels to help traders and investors study planetary aspects.

You have probably experienced the effects of the planets on the financial market without even realizing it. Consider the following examples:

The financial media issued numerous dire predictions for financial market calamity following the 2016 election of Donald Trump to the White House. When the S&P 500 instead responded by powering higher, analysts were flummoxed. What they failed to realize was that Mercury was near its heliocentric declination low and near 0-degrees of geocentric latitude. Venus was near its latitude low. Moon was at its declination low point. Heliocentric Mercury and Saturn were making a 0-degree conjunction.

The S&P 500 hit a rough patch in 2018 from October through year end. The official story centered around the Federal Reserve raising its key lending rate too quickly. Also at issue was trade tensions with China starting to heat up. Fuelling the steep correction was heliocentric Venus making a 0-degree conjunction to Earth along with heliocentric Mercury making a 0-degree conjunction to Saturn. In addition, Mercury was at its declination low and Moon was at its declination maximum. The market weakness ended as heliocentric Saturn made a 180-degree aspect to Earth.

U.S. equity markets peaked in late February 2020 and went into a spasm in March 2020 when fears of the potential for a viral pandemic were stirred up. At the time, heliocentric Mercury was at its closest approach to the Sun (perihelion) while at the same time passing conjunct to Earth. The conjunct pair were 120-degrees trine to Jupiter as well. In addition, Mercury and Venus were both at their declination maxima. Moon was at its declination minimum.

Remember the confusion surrounding the November 2020 election of Joe Biden to the White House? In the closing days of the campaign, Earth was 90-degrees square to Jupiter and Saturn (which were conjunct to one another); Venus had just completed a 180-degree opposition to the Jupiter and Saturn, and Moon was at its declination maximum.

The events of late 2021 reminded us all again of the power of planetary events. As 2021 was ending, both the Nasdaq 100 and S&P 500 the equity markets were peaking. Russian troops were massing on the border with Ukraine. Moon was at its declination maximum. Heliocentric Venus was 0-degrees conjunct to Earth which in turn was 120-degrees trine to Jupiter and square to Mercury as well. This was a powerful concentration of cosmic energy bearing down on human emotion. The powerful players (whoever they were) took full advantage, pushing the markets into a downtrend through aggressive selling. Individual investors (whose emotions were rattled by news events) panicked and started selling which fed into the downtrend. By June 2022, the selling had caused a 20% decline across equity markets. On the day the selling stopped, there were no aspects between Mercury, Venus, Earth, Jupiter, or Saturn to influence human emotion.

The equity markets hit another serious patch of turbulence in April 2025 when the Trump administration levied steep tariffs against the rest of the world. Both heliocentric Mercury and Venus made 0-degree conjunctions to Earth during this sell-off. Moon recorded its declination maximum as well.

As these examples suggest, this edition of the *Financial Astrology Almanac* marks a radical departure in analytical technique. Ever since launching the annual *Financial Astrology Almanac* publication in 2014, the focus has been on classical, geocentric astrology. In past Almanac editions, the narrative was centered around empirical evidence that showed how events of planets passing by key points in the first trade horoscope wheels of financial exchanges and passing by key points in the IPO (first trade date) horoscope wheels of commodity futures instruments aligned to price trend changes. In this edition, focus will not be on empirical classical astrology, but rather on physical planetary events.

This edition mainly embraces the work of astronomers and mathematicians such as Scafetta, Tattersall, and Wilson. These brilliant minds have amassed statistical data that points to Mercury, Venus, Earth, Jupiter, and Saturn exerting gravitational and inertial torque forces on the surface layers of the Sun. These forces are amplified by up to 4 million times when these planets make angles of 0, 90, 120, and 180-degrees to one another. These torque forces exacerbate the production of solar particle emissions which are only partly deflected away from Earth by its surrounding geomagnetic field. These researchers have also compiled statistical evidence that shows that these particle emissions affect the momentum of upper atmospheric winds which in turn affect weather patterns. Their findings also point to the declination of the Moon as playing a role in upper atmospheric variability.

By extension of their research findings, this edition of the Almanac suggests that these forces are also amplified when these planets are at extremes of latitude and declination. This Almanac takes the position that if torque forces and solar emissions are capable of affecting our weather, then they are also capable of affecting human emotion. It is variations in human emotion that in turn drive the financial markets.

These researchers have also determined that our solar system functions with resonance. Axial spin times and orbital times of Mercury, Venus, and Earth bear a mathematical relation to one another. This edition of the Almanac presents the reader with the dominant mathematically-determined cycles that influence price action on indices and commodity futures instruments. These cycles are closely related to the orbital and axial spin times of Mercury, Venus, and Earth.

Despite the obvious correlation between market price action and planetary movements, the North American investor remains largely unaware of how planetary movements and cycles influence human emotion and market volatility. There are, however, powerful players in the world's major financial centres who *do* embrace planetary movements and cycles. These players use this planetary knowledge to control the markets all while showering individual investors with analyst opinion, distracting press releases, and unproven academic theories.

My goal in all of the writing that I do remains unchanged: to explain to traders and investors that the key to understanding the financial markets is to view them through the lens of planetary activity. I sincerely hope that this Almanac (which is my thirteenth such annual publication) will help to take your trading and investing activity to a new level as you navigate the markets during 2026.

**Note from the Author:** I am also the author of several other astrology books and publish two bi-weekly subscription-based newsletters called *The Astrology Letter* and *The Cycle Report.* In addition, I host a Substack channel (@PlanetaryTrader). Through all of my efforts, I hope to encourage people to embrace the events in our cosmos as valuable tools to aid in trading and investing decision making.

# CHAPTER ONE

## *Fundamentals*

When considering the planetary motion that defines our solar system, there are two 'planes' to consider: the *ecliptic plane* and the *celestial equator plane*. The planets in our solar system (Mercury, Venus, Mars, Jupiter, Saturn, Uranus, Neptune, and Pluto) orbit 360-degrees around the Sun following a path called the *ecliptic plane*. Projecting the Earth's equator into space produces the celestial equator plane. There are two points of intersection between the ecliptic plane and celestial equator plane. Mathematically, this makes sense as two non-parallel planes must intersect at two points. These points are commonly called the *vernal equinox* (occurring around March 20$^{th}$) and the *autumnal equinox* (occurring around September 20$^{th}$). At the vernal equinox, the Sun is at 0-degrees of the sign of Aries. The vernal equinox denotes the first day of Spring. At the autumnal equinox, the Sun is at 0-degrees of Libra. The autumnal equinox denotes the first day of Autumn.

## The Zodiac Wheel

Philosophers and high priests in ancient civilizations divided the night sky into twelve segments. They assigned names to groupings of stars in these segments and watched as the five planets visible to the naked eye (Mercury, Venus, Mars, Jupiter, Saturn) moved relative to these patterns of stars. These planetary movements became steeped in mythology and symbolism. Today, the symbolism is still with us.

The positions of planets relative to the twelve segments of the sky can be expressed in 2-dimensions by plotting them on a circular image called a *zodiac wheel.* The starting point (or zero-degree point) of a zodiac wheel is at 0-degrees of the sign Aries. The wheel comprises twelve segments (signs) of 30-degrees each. Each sign is denoted by a symbol (called a glyph). Figure 1-1 illustrates the glyphs that denote the twelve segments of a zodiac wheel. The various planets represented on the zodiac wheel are also denoted by glyphs, as shown in Figure 1-2.

**Figure 1-1**
The Zodiac Wheel

There is no shortage of books available that connect a planet's position in the various zodiac signs to deeper psychological meanings. These connections are purely empirical and have been collected over the years by astrologers and counsellors. Notable among these people was 1960s French psychologist Michel Gauquelin. His work helped pave the way for classical geocentric astrology.

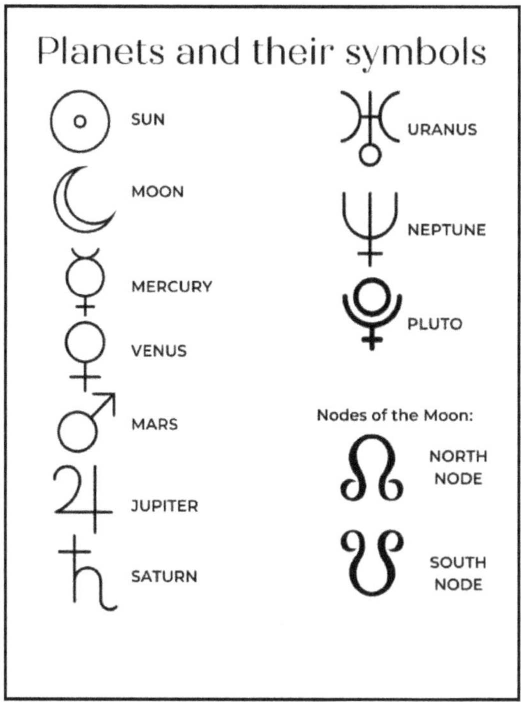


**Figure 1-2**
The Glyphs

## Geocentric and Heliocentric Astrology

There are two distinct ways of plotting planetary locations on a zodiac wheel – geocentric and heliocentric. In *geocentric* astrology, the Earth is the vantage point for observing the planets as they pass through the signs of the zodiac. In *heliocentric* astrology, the Sun is the vantage point for observing the planets as they pass through the signs of the zodiac.

This Almanac focuses on heliocentric planetary locations; more specifically those of Mercury, Venus, Earth, Jupiter, and Saturn.

## Data

To identify aspects between planets, astrologers often use Ephemeris tables. For geocentric astrology, the *New American Ephemeris for the 21st Century* is commonly used. For heliocentric astrology, the *American Heliocentric Ephemeris* is a good resource.

As an alternative to using tabular data in an Ephemeris book, a quicker aspect determination can be made using software. An excellent, although expensive, software program for generating zodiac wheels is *Solar Fire Gold* produced by software company Astrolabe. An end-of-day charting program that allows the user to overlay planetary phenomenon and cycle studies onto price charts is the *Optuma* software program. As your journey into trading and investing using the planets deepens, you might be tempted to spend the money to acquire one or both of these software programs.

## Latitude

As the planets make their respective journeys around the Sun, forces of gravitational attraction between them and the Sun cause a movement above and below the celestial equator plane (as viewed from our vantage point here on Earth). This movement is called *latitude*. The larger, outer planets (Jupiter, Saturn, Neptune, Uranus and Pluto), which are more distant from the Sun, experience smaller gravitational forces and hence exhibit latitude changes of smaller amplitude.

The smaller, inner planets (Mercury, Venus, Earth) exhibit greater amplitude and more frequent latitude changes.

## Longitude

The position of a planet in the zodiac is expressed in degrees relative to 0-degrees of Aries. For example, a planet at 0-degrees of Capricorn is said to be at 270-degrees of *longitude.* A combination of longitude and latitude can be used to define the geocentric coordinate location of a planet in our solar system.

## Declination

To an observer at a fixed reference point in space such as the Sun, the planets can be seen orbiting the 360-degrees around the Sun following the ecliptic plane. As the planets make their orbital journeys, gravitational forces cause them to move above and below the ecliptic plane. This movement is called *declination.*

## Right Ascension

The zodiac wheel comprises 360 degrees. There are 24 hours in one Earth day. This means there are 15 zodiac degrees in each hour (15 degrees x 24 hours = 360 zodiac degrees). Expressing a planet's zodiac location in terms of hours is called *Right Ascension.* A combination of Right Ascension and declination can be used to define the heliocentric coordinates of a planet in the three-dimensional cosmos.

## The Moon

Just as the planets orbit 360-degrees around the Sun, the Moon orbits 360-degrees around the Earth in a plane of motion called the *lunar ecliptic plane.* This plane is inclined at about 5-degrees to the ecliptic plane. The Moon orbits Earth with a slight elliptical pattern in approximately 27.3 days, relative to an observer located on a fixed frame of reference such as the Sun. This time period is known as a *sidereal month.* To an observer located on Earth (a moving frame of reference) the Moon will appear to take slightly longer to orbit the planet. An Earth-bound observer will see a complete orbit of the Moon around the Earth in approximately 29.5 days (one New Moon to the next New Moon). This 29.5-day period of time is known as a *synodic month* or more commonly a *lunar* month.

## The Nodes

The North and South nodes are the geocentric points of intersection between the Earth's ecliptic plane and the Moon's ecliptic plane. In financial astrology, typically only the North Node is referred to. In 18.6 years, the North Node point will make a complete journey through all twelve signs of the zodiac. To ancient civilizations, the 18.6-year period was important because it correlated to maximum declination. That is, every 18.6 years, the Moon in the northern hemisphere could be seen rising and setting at extreme points in the sky. Many megalithic archeological sites around the world are oriented to observe this maximum declination.

## Synodic and Sidereal

The concepts of synodic and sidereal extend beyond the Moon to include all the planets. To an Earth-bound observer, a synodic time period is the time between two successive planetary occurrences. For example, how many days does it take for Sun passing Pluto on the zodiac wheel to Sun again passing Pluto?

To a Sun-bound observer (a fixed frame of reference), a sidereal time period is the number of days (or years) it takes for a planet to orbit the Sun one time. The data in the following table presents synodic and sidereal times.

| PLANET | SYNODIC PERIOD | SIDEREAL PERIOD |
|---|---|---|
| Mercury | 116 days | 88 days |
| Venus | 584 days | 225 days |
| Mars | 780 days | 1.9 years |
| Jupiter | 399 days | 11.9 years |
| Saturn | 378 days | 29.5 years |
| Uranus | 370 days | 84 years |
| Neptune | 368 days | 164.8 years |
| Pluto | 367 days | 248.5 years |

**Figure 1-3**
Synodic and Sidereal Times

For planets closer to the Sun, the formula to determine the synodic cycle between them is: 1/S = 1/P -1/E ; where S is the synodic period, P is the sidereal period of the planet in question and E is synodic period of the second planet. For example, the synodic period of Mercury and Earth is: 1/S = 1/88 – 1/365. S calculates as 116 days.

## Aspects

Owing to the different times for the planets to each orbit the Sun, an observer situated on Earth will see the planets making distinct angles (called *geocentric aspects*) with one another and also with the Sun. An observer situated at a fixed reference point, such as the Sun, will see the planets making distinct angles (called *heliocentric aspects*) with one another and also with the Earth. In financial astrology, it is common to refer to only the 0, 90, 120 and 180-degree aspects.

## Retrograde

The term *retrograde* is taken from the Latin expression *retrogradus* which means "backward step". From our vantage point on Earth, there will be three times during a year when Earth and Mercury pass by each other. Once each year, Earth and Venus will pass each other. As a faster-moving planet starts to lap past slower-moving Earth, we can observe the faster-planet's position relative to one of the star constellations in the sky. Owing to the different orbital speeds of Earth and the faster planet, there will be a period of time when we see the faster planet in what appears to be the previous constellation. For example, we might start off seeing Mercury against the star constellation of Gemini. As Mercury begins to lap past Earth, we will see Mercury against the star constellation of Taurus. As Mercury passes by Earth, we will see Mercury again in Taurus. Of course, Mercury has not physically reversed course and moved backwards. This is an optical illusion created by the different orbital speeds of Mercury and Earth.

These brief illusory periods are what astrologers call *retrograde* events. To ancient societies, retrograde events were of great significance as human emotion was often seen to be changeable at these events. Retrograde events involving Mercury and Venus very often lead to short term price trend changes developing across markets.

To an observer on a fixed vantage point in space, times when heliocentric Mercury or Venus pass 0-degrees conjunct to Earth are equivalent to the retrograde period witnessed by the Earth-bound observer using geocentric astrology.

## Superior and Inferior Conjunctions

Mercury and Venus are closer to the Sun than is the Earth. From our vantage point on Earth, there will be times when Mercury and

Venus are situated between the Earth and the Sun. There will also be times when the Sun is between the Earth and Mercury or between Earth and Venus.

On a geocentric zodiac wheel, an *inferior conjunction* occurs when retrograde Mercury or Venus is 0-degrees conjunct the Sun. A s*uperior conjunction* occurs when the Sun is conjunct to non-retrograde Mercury or Venus.

On the heliocentric zodiac wheel, the times when Mercury or Venus are at inferior conjunction will have these planets 0-degrees conjunct to Earth. The times when Mercury or Venus are at superior conjunction will have these planets 180-degreees opposite to Earth.

After Venus has been at inferior conjunction, it will be visible in the early morning hours as the *Morning Star*. After it has been at superior conjunction, it will be visible just before sunset as the *Evening Star.*

Venus was at Superior Conjunction on March 28, 2013 (8 Aries), October 25, 2014 (1 Scorpio), June 6, 2016 (16 Gemini), January 8, 2018 (18 Capricorn), August 14, 2019 (20 Leo), March 26, 2021 (6 Aries), October 22, 2022 (28 Libra), June 4, 2024 (15 Gemini), and January 6, 2026 (16 Capricorn).

Venus was at Inferior Conjunction on June 6, 2012 (15 Gemini), January 11, 2014 (21 Capricorn), August 15, 2015 (22 Leo), March 25, 2017 (4 Aries), October 26, 2018 (3 Scorpio), June 3, 2020 (14 Gemini), January 8, 2022 (19 Capricorn), and August 13, 2023 (20 Leo), March 22, 2025 (2 Aries) and October 23, 2026 (0 Scorpio).

If one plots consecutive superior conjunction events (or consecutive inferior conjunction events) on a zodiac wheel, successive conjunction points can be joined to form a 5-pointed star called a *pentagram*. Such is the elegance and mystique of the cosmos.

## Helion Events

From an observer's vantage point on a fixed reference point in space, there will also be times when Mercury and Venus are closest to or farthest away from the Sun. Times of being closest to the Sun are termed *perihelion* events. Times of being farthest away from the Sun are termed *aphelion* events.

Venus has an orbit that is only slightly elliptical. When Venus is nearer to the Sun it is about 107.4 million kms away. When Venus is farthest from the Sun it is about 109 million kms away. Despite this small difference (109 versus 107.4 million kms), Venus helion events can still be seen to occasionally have an effect on human emotion and the markets.

Mercury has an eccentric orbit in which its distance from the Sun will range from 46 million km to 70 million km. When Mercury is nearer to the Sun (46 million kms away), it is moving at its fastest (56.6 km per second). When Mercury is farther from the Sun (70 million km away), it is moving slower (38.7 km per second). Mercury helion events very often have an effect on human emotion and the markets.

## Apogee and Perigee Events

There will be times when Moon is closest to or farthest away from the Earth. Times of Moon being closest to the Sun are termed *perigee* events. Times of Moon being farthest away from the Sun are termed *apogee* events. At apogee, the Moon is approximately 405,000 kms away from Earth. At perigee it is approximately 363,000 kms away from Earth.

## Spatial Distribution

The Sun is at the center of our solar system, with the Earth, Moon, and eight other planets completing the planetary system. Mercury is the closest of all the planes to the Sun. Pluto is the farthest away. Mercury orbits one time around the Sun in 88 days. Pluto takes just over 248 years.

The distances of the planets from the Sun are cited in *astronomical units* (au), where 1 au is defined as the distance from Earth to the Sun (approximately 150 million km). The distances of the planets from the Sun are : Mercury (0.4 au), Venus (0.79 au), Earth (1 au), Mars (1.5 au), Jupiter (5.2 au), Saturn (9.5 au), Uranus (19.2 au), Neptune (30.06 au), and Pluto (39 au).

Closer examination of the ratios of these distances to one another reveals that the ratio of Venus' distance to Mercury's distance is very close to the number 2. The ratio of Jupiter's distance to Mercury's distance is very nearly 13. The ratio of Saturn's distance to Mercury's distance is very close to 21. The ratio of The ratio of Pluto's distance to Mercury's distance is very close to 89. These are all numbers that comprise the *Fibonacci sequence*. Spatial relations between planets that closely align to the Fibonacci sequence is a humbling phenomenon that leads one to the observation that our solar system is nor random. It is ordered in a grand design which has been created by a higher power. Some people might label this higher power as *God*. Others might apply the label *Allah*. Freemasonic thinkers refer to the higher power as *The Great Architect of the Universe*.

# CHAPTER TWO

## *Fibonacci*

If the planets in our solar system are spatially distributed in a grand design that closely follows the Fibonacci sequence, this begs the questions: what is a Fibonacci sequence? Who was Fibonacci?

Leonardo Pisano Bigollo (1180-1250) was the son of Bonacci Bigollo, an Italian trader and businessman. In the Italian language of the day, *filius* was the word for "son of ". Leonardo came to be known as filius Bonacci or son of Bonacci. This word play ended up as Fibonacci.

As a young lad, Fibonacci went on many journeys with his father to the major Mediterranean trading ports in north Africa. On these adventures he overheard many conversations between traders and merchants. He learned that traders were using one of two numbering systems: the Roman numeral system and the Hindu-Arabic system.

The Roman numeral system, which traces its origins to circa 900 B.C. was based on figures from the Latin alphabet. For example, the figure "V" denoted the number 5. The figure "IV" denoted one less than 5, which is 4. Young Leonardo observed that this system was difficult to work with. For example, IV + V = IX (4 + 5 = 9) was not intuitive.

The Hindu Arabic system, which traces its origins back to circa 200 B.C. was based on the values 0,1,2,3,4,5,6,7,8,9. As Figure 2-1 shows, the numerical value of the individual figures in this numbering system denotes the number of angles in a particular figure. For example, the figure that we recognize as our number 2 contains two distinct angles. The figure that we recognize as our number 3 contains three angles. The figure that we recognize as our number 7 contains seven angles.

**Figure 2-1**
Angles and the basis for our numbering system

Intrigued with the Hindu Arabic system, and intrigued with the conversations he overheard amongst traders and merchants, young Leonardo examined the Hindu Arabic system's numerical values and their additive properties. Consider the numerical values of 1,2,3,5, and 8:

- Starting with 0 and 1 and adding them, he arrived at 1 (0 + 1 = 1).
- Taking 0,1,1, he added the last two digits and arrived at 2 (1 + 1 = 2).
- Taking 0,1,1,2, he added the last two digits and arrived at 3 (1 + 2 = 3).
- Taking 0,1,1,2,3, he added the last two digits to get 5. (2 + 3 = 5).
- Taking 0,1,1,2,3,5 he added the last two digits to get 8. (3 + 5 = 8).

A sequence of numbers in which a given term of the sequence is the sum of the two numbers preceding is called a *recursive sequence.* He then turned his attention to a fascinating feature of the recursive sequence. He observed that a term of the sequence when divided by the term immediately before it produced a result very close to 1.618. For example, consider the following terms of Fibonacci's recursive sequence with each term divided by the term before it:

377 / 233 = 1.618
233 / 144 = 1.618
144 / 89 = 1.618
89 / 55 = 1.618
55 / 34 = 1.617

But what was 1.618?

Consider the image of a rectangle in Figure 2-2. The right end of the rectangle has had a line drawn through it to form a square with sides of dimension 1. The remainder of the long side of the rectangle measures "x".

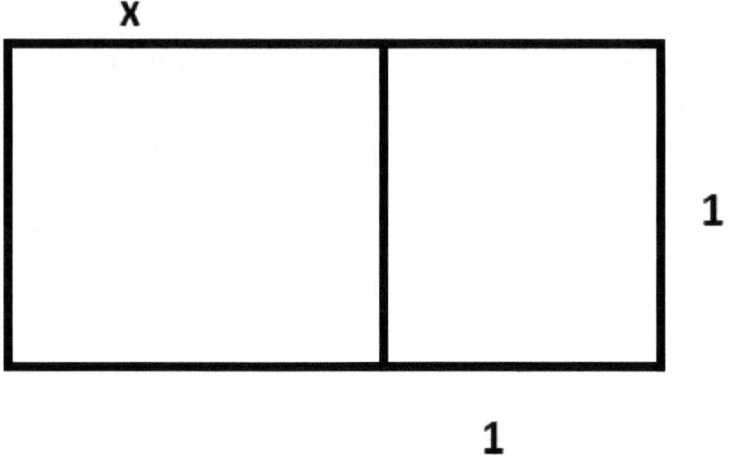


**Figure 2-2**
Proportions

The long side of the rectangle (x + 1 in length) divided by "x", is proportional to "x" divided by 1. This is expressed by the formula:

$x + 1 / x = x / 1.$

Arranging this expression into an algebraic equation gives:

$x2 - x - 1 = 0$

$x = (1 + \sqrt{5})/2$

$x = 1.618$

This was not Fibonacci's discovery. The ancient Greek's were aware of square root mathematics and also of 1.618 which they incorporated into their art, sculpting, and architecture. So enamored were they with 1.618 that they assigned it the Greek letter *phi.*

Today, the recursive sequence that young Leonardo had become aware of is commonly called the Fibonacci sequence. Market strategists have taken phi (1.618) and performed some inverse square root operations on it as follows:

$(1/\sqrt{1.618}) = 0.786$
$((1/\sqrt{1.618}))^2 = 0.618$
$((1/\sqrt{1.618}))^3 = 0.486$
$((1/\sqrt{1.618}))^4 = 0.382$
$((1/\sqrt{1.618}))^6 = 0.236$

Traders and investors call these values *Fibonacci retracements.* Fibonacci retracement levels can be seen time and again when examining price charts of stocks, commodities, and major indices. For example, a bullish move higher in price might be followed by a retracement during which profits are taken. The retracement will practically always be one of the Fibonacci retracements. The same can also be seen following a bearish decline. As short sellers take long positions to cover off their short positions, the retracement in price as a fraction of the original bearish move will practically always align to one of these Fibonacci retracement values. The chart of Gold futures in Figure 2-3 illustrates how two Fibonacci 61.8% retracements occurred between March and May 2025.

**Figure 2-3**
Gold futures and Fibonacci

As a further illustration of the recursive property of phi, consider the following mathematical operations using 1.618. These are what traders and investors call Fibonacci extensions:

$(1.618)^1 = 1.618$
$(1.618)^2 = 2.618$
$(1.618)^3 = 4.236$
$(1.618)^4 = 6.854$

Notice that 4.236 is the sum of 2.618 and 1.618. Note too that 6.854 is the sum of 4.236 plus 2.618. Occasionally, one will see these extensions on a price chart.

The chart in Figure 2-4 illustrates price action on the E-mini S&P 500 which declined between July and October 2023. The rally that followed was a 2.618 times extension of the decline. After an orderly 23.6% fade, the market then rallied by a 2.618 times extension of the decline amount into July 2024.

**Figure 2-4**
S&P 500 and Fibonacci (2023-2024)

The chart in Figure 2-5 illustrates price action in 2025. The rally that followed the April 2025 selloff continued into late October 2025 and was a 1.618 times multiple of the April 2025 selloff.

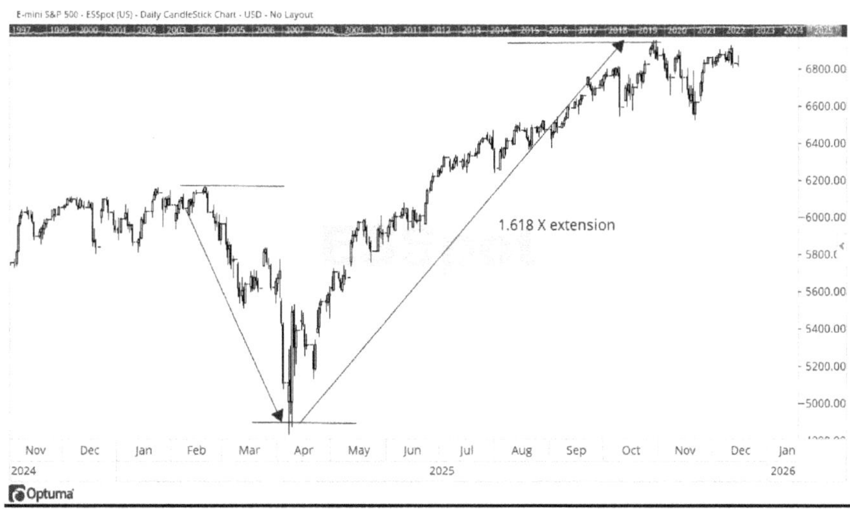


**Figure 2-5**
Figure 2-5 S&P 500 and Fibonacci (2024-2025)

# CHAPTER THREE

## *Planetary Resonance*

Pythagoras of Samos (570–495 B.C.) intuitively felt that the visible planets were synchronized in their journeys through the night sky. He called this phenomenon *musica universalis* (music of the spheres). However, that is as close as he could come to quantifying his intuitions given his rudimentary understanding of the planets.

A couple centuries later Greek philosopher Eudoxus of Cnidus advanced the idea that the Earth is at the center of the universe and all other celestial bodies rotate around the Earth. Astronomers now refer to this model as the *geocentric model.* This model remained dominant for 1,800 years until Prussian mathematician and astronomer Nicolaus Copernicus wrote *De Revolutionibus Orbium Coelestium* (On the Revolutions of the Heavenly Spheres) in 1543. In this groundbreaking work he described the *heliocentric model* in which the planets make circular orbits around the Sun. He also claimed that the planets Mercury, Venus, Earth, Mars, Jupiter and Saturn were not randomly distributed; they followed an ordered pattern. But he was unable to describe what the pattern looked like.

In 1596, German mathematician and astronomer Johannes Kepler advanced the work of Copernicus when he wrote *Mysterium Cosmographicum* (The Cosmographic Mystery) in which he described Mercury, Venus, Earth, Mars, Jupiter and Saturn as having a proportion amongst them. Kepler believed that God had created this proportion and he set about trying to find a mathematical model to describe the proportion. He felt the Sun was representative of God and that the Sun provided a motive force to make the planets orbit around it. After much study, he concluded that the planets orbit the Sun in elliptical patterns where the Sun is one of the two focal points in a given planet's elliptical pattern.

The proportion between planets received further support in 1766 when German astronomer Johann Daniel Titius unveiled a formula for describing the distance of a given planet from the Sun. This formula was further advanced in 1772 by German mathematician Johann Elert Bode. This formula came to be known as the *Titius Bode Law.* While the formula was not pinpoint precise, it further advanced the idea that there was a proportional relationship between the planets.

As discussed in the previous chapter, astronomers have now recognized that the spatial distribution between planets is related to the Fibonacci sequence. In addition, they have recognized other patterns. For example, the ratio between the Earth's orbital radius around the Sun (defined as 1 astronomical unit or 1 au) and Venus' orbital radius (0.72 au) is very close to the ratio between the diagonal and the side of a square having a side dimension of 1 unit. The *Pythagorean Theorem* says that in this square, $1^2 + 1^2 = c^2$. Solving for c gives $c=\sqrt{2}$ or 1.41. The actual ratio of 1 au to 0.72 au is 1.39. As another example, the ratio between Saturn's orbital radius (a = 9.5 au) and Jupiter's orbital radius (a = 5.2 au) which calculates to 1.82 is approximately equivalent to the ratio between the diagonal and the side of a cube (√3 or 1.73). The dimensional relations between planets extend beyond squares and cubes. The orbital periods and axial spin times of planets also bear some strong relations.

The mathematical relation between planetary movements is what astronomers call *resonance*. Consider the following numerous examples that illustrate the resonance in our cosmos:

- Jupiter travels around the Sun approximately five times in the time it takes for two orbits of Saturn. Every 60 years, Jupiter and Saturn will meet at the same point in the zodiac wheel.
- Venus rotates on its axis 28 times while Mercury completes 116 rotations about its axis. This is very close to a 4 : 1 ratio (4 x 28 = 112).
- One axial rotation of Mercury (58.65 days) is 2/3 of its 88 day orbit around the Sun. A total of 116 rotations takes 6,803 days. Venus rotates about its axis once in 243 days. A total of 28 rotations takes 6,804 days. Not only are these two timeframes nearly identical but 116 + 28 = 144, a Fibonacci number.
- In the time it takes for Venus and Mercury to be conjunct on 28 occasions, Venus will orbit the Sun 18 times and Mercury will orbit the Sun 46 times. The timeframe for these 28 conjunctions is just over 11 years, the average length of a sunspot cycle.
- Venus spins about its axis one time in 243 days. During the time it takes for Venus to go from being conjunct Jupiter to again being conjunct Jupiter, Venus will spin on its axis 1.03 times. During the time it takes for Earth to go from being conjunct Jupiter to again being conjunct Jupiter, Earth will

spin 399 times about its axis. The ratio 399 to 1.03 is very close to a 400:1 ratio.

- Venus spins about its axis once in 243 days. Earth rotates around the Sun once in 365 days. Venus' rotation is in a 3 : 2 relationship with Earth's orbital period. Three axial spins of Venus (3 x 243 = 729 days) equate very closely to two Earth orbits around the Sun (365 x 2 = 730 days).
- 50 geocentric Sun-Mars synodic periods equal 106.76 years. This is identical to nine orbits of Jupiter around the Sun (11.86 years x 9 = 106.76 years).
- 37 geocentric Sun-Mars synodic cycles equal 79.0025 years. This is very close to 79 orbits of Earth around the Sun = 79 years.
- The ratio of Venus axial spin time (243 days) to its orbital period (225 days) is 1.08. The ratio of Earth's axial spin rate to its orbital period equals 0.0027. These figures are in the ratio of 400:1.

There are many more examples cited in scientific literature. The key observation is that our solar system is more complex than we can imagine. The resonance in our solar system has profound effects on our planet.

## Gravitational Torque

In the early 1950s, a little-known Russian astrophysicist who was working on Soviet hydrogen bomb experiments arrived at an unorthodox idea concerning solar luminance. His work, which followed on the theories expounded by Albert Einstein, was apparently so ground-breaking that the Soviet authorities removed him (and his work) from having any further contact with the outside scientific world. His name – Dr. Nikolai Kozyrev. His idea was that space-time itself is a source of torsional (torque) energy. The energy is intensified at various times due to the spatial heliocentric geometries (aspects) of the planets. This energy then causes the rotating plasma of the Sun to become a giant torsional machine, but one with predictability because the heliocentric positions of the planets are known at any given moment.

In 1974, British researchers King and Willis arrived at the idea that changes in the Earth's magnetic field create changes in meteorological pressures which influence weather patterns. However, the two were unable to identify the exact mechanism. Astronomers have since come to realize that it is *constructive resonance* that transfers gravitational torque and inertia to the surface layers of the Sun which in turn results in meteorological changes.

In 1984, Columbia University professor R.W. Fairbridge summed up the effects of gravitational torque:

1. Large planets Saturn and Jupiter transmit gravitational torque waves which cause changes to the velocity and spin rate of the various planets as well as of the Sun. These changes manifest on Earth in terms of seismic and volcanic activity.
2. Gravitational torque waves imparted to the Sun manifest in terms of sunspots and greater electromagnetic particle emission, both of which impact the geomagnetic field of the Earth as "solar wind".
3. The affected geomagnetic field generates reactions within the Earth's upper atmosphere which induces weather pattern changes.

Swedish astronomer N.A. Mörner has added to the argument with his opinion that changes in solar wind emission velocity vary between about 400 km per second and 750 km per second. Because the shielding capacity of the Earth's magnetosphere cannot withstand this variability, the flux of cosmic radiation hitting Earth and its inhabitants will vary markedly. Mörner is also of the opinion that the interaction between cosmic radiation and the Earth's magnetosphere causes small changes in the Earth's spin rate. These changes translate into atmospheric pressure fluctuations and even perturbations in ocean currents.

Gravitational torque influencing the Sun has been studied through solar irradiance examinations. The scientific community generally accepts that the average irradiance (brightness) of the Sun is 1361 Watts per square meter ($W/m^2$). In 1967, Australian researcher E.K. Bigg studied the short-term variations in solar irradiance around a baseline of this average. He noted a cyclicality in the data he collected. His conclusion was that the irradiance displayed two cycles: a 24.8-day cycle and a 34.3-day cycle. He concluded that these cycle times must be related to the rotational period of parts of the Sun. Astronomers have now proven him correct. The region of the Sun near its poles spins axially one time in about 34-35 days. The region of the Sun at its equatorial mid-section spins axially one time in about 25 days.

Italian astronomer Nicola Scafetta has since expanded on Bigg's work and determined that a 24.8-day cycle arises due to the gravitational torque resulting from aspects between Jupiter and Venus. He is also of the opinion that a 34.3-day cycle is influenced by the gravitational torque coming from aspects between Jupiter and Mercury.

Bigg also noted medium-term cycles in irradiance of 5.43 years and 8.34 years. He mathematically showed these periods to be related to the orbital periods of Venus, Earth, Jupiter, and Saturn:

Cycle Length = $(2/Pv - 3/Pe - 2/Pj + 3/Ps)^{-1}$ = 5.43 years.
Cycle Length = $2 \times (1/Pv + 2/Pe - 2/Pj + 1/Ps)^{-1}$ = 8.34 years.

Scafetta has also come to conclude that when Mercury, Venus, Earth, Jupiter, or Saturn make angles of 0, 90, 120, or 180 degrees with one another, the gravitational torque forces exacted on the surface layers of the Sun are at a maximum. Therefore, these hard angles tie directly to Morner's idea of cosmic ray variability and Bigg's irradiance studies.

Knowing that the orbits of these four planets affect solar irradiance, a study of a weekly price chart will reveal if the irradiance changes affect the financial markets. Figure 3-1 illustrates the 5.43 year (282 week) cycle fitted to the S&P 500 using a start point of the early 2009 significant market lows. Also fitted to this price chart is the 8.34-year cycle using a start point of the 2000 market high.

The 8.34 year cycle aligns to the end of the 2008 market selloff as well as to the April 2025 trading tariff impositions that made investors nervous. The 8.34-year cycle should have produced a market response in 2016, but it did not. Recall that at the time, the Federal Reserve was powering full-steam ahead with its quantitative easing program which fueled an almost insatiable bullish attitude. Note how the end points of the 5.43 year cycle very closely align to the 2020 COVID panic event as well as the April 2025 equity market lows. This implies that in late 2030 there should be a market response when the cycle terminates again.

**Figure 3-1**
S&P 500 and the 5.43 year and 8.34 year cycles

Figure 3-2 illustrates the 5.43 year (282 week) cycle fitted to a weekly chart of Soybean futures. The starting point for both cycle overlays is the price lows of 2001. Note how the end points of both cycles align to price swing points.

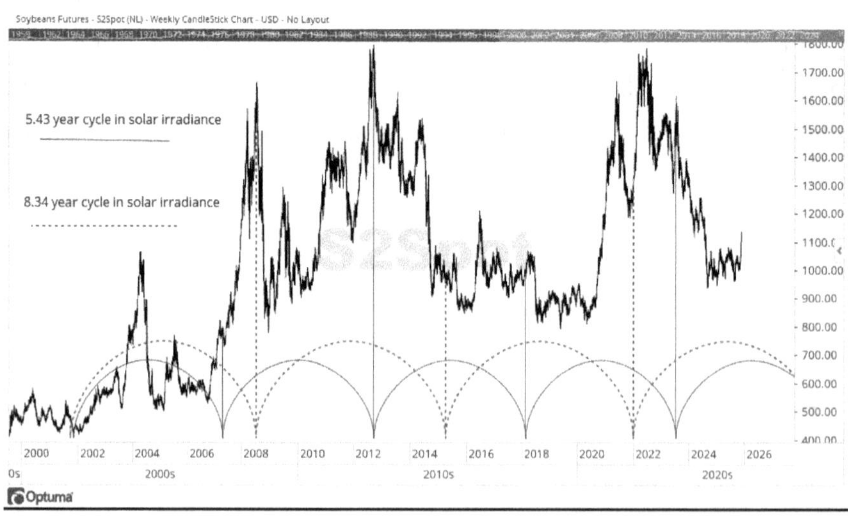


**Figure 3-2**
Soybeans and the 5.43 year and 8.34 year cycles

The key observation in these two examples is that there is a connection between solar and planetary events and the financial markets. The work of astronomers such as Bigg, Fairbridge, Scafetta, and Morner can be extended to explain price variability on the financial markets. Variability in both solar irradiance and solar wind emissions influences human emotion which in turn influences the propensity of people to buy or sell.

## Emotions

As to how our emotions are affected, there is still much that scientists have not figured out. However, one mechanism that is understood is the *Sodium-Potassium model.* This model was discovered in 1957 by Danish scientist Jens Christian Skou. Our brain cells normally have a concentration gradient of more positively charged sodium ions ($Na^+$) outside the cell walls and a concentration gradient of more positively charged potassium ions ($K^+$) inside the cell walls. On balance, the electric charge inside the cells is negative (between 40 and 90 millivolts). A stimulus event, such as an increase in electromagnetic particles hitting the human body, will cause a cellular reaction in which ion channels open and $Na^+$ ions move out of the cells and K+ ions move into the cells. This ion exchange then triggers a cascade of cellular events through the brain, including the uptake of glucose and amino acids into brain cells. After the stimulus event has subsided, the ion gradients will return to their starting configurations. It is very likely then that this cascade of cellular events is what can be referred to as an emotional change.

Another cellular mechanism that may interface with emotional change involves cryptochrome receptors. A human brain cell generates cellular energy via the Krebs Cycle. In the final stage of this cycle, electrons from the inner mitochondrial cell membrane pass through the electron transport chain where they come in contact with specialized flavoprotein receptors. The released electron energy pushes protons ($H^+$ ions) into contact with an enzyme to produce cellular energy. The final step in the electron transport chain is the electron meeting an oxygen receptor molecule. The resulting reduction reaction transforms the molecular oxygen into water ($H_2O$). However, if the brain cell in question is subjected to a change in electromagnetic field (as a result of increased solar particle emissions from the Sun), the oxygen-proton reaction can become compromised. The oxygen molecule will transform into what is termed a *reactive oxygen species* (ROS). The ROS product will induce a change in the cell's normal signaling ability. This change is what can be referred to as an emotional change.

## Cycles

There are more cycles in play than just those identified by E.K. Bigg. At first glance, price charts of stocks, commodities, and indices appear to lack distinct patterns. However, behind the up and down price movements are cyclical patterns not immediately apparent to the naked eye. These patterns can be revealed using a *Periodogram function.*

The math behind the Periodogram function is complex and is based on work of 18th century mathematical genius Jean-Baptiste Joseph Fourier. Born in France in 1768, Fourier was educated by Benedictine monks. His brilliance eventually led him to be appointed the scientific advisor to Napoleon Bonaparte. Among his many mathematical achievements, Fourier developed a complex equation which could be used to reveal the frequencies present in a linear time series of data.

Today, some financial data software platforms (such as the Optuma software program) have a Periodogram algorithm built in. With the click of a mouse, one can readily determine the frequencies that are the most dominant in the price chart.

In preparing this manuscript, back-testing of price data for various commodity futures contracts, indices, and individual stocks showed that there are indeed dominant cycles in the price data. At first glance, these dominant cycles appeared to be random numbers. However, closer examination of the cycle lengths showed they were closely related to heliocentric celestial body phenomena such as the Mercury orbital period (88 days), the Mercury axial spin time (58.65 days), the Venus orbital period (225 days), the Venus axial spin time (243 days), the Earth orbital period (365 days), and in a couple cases the Mars orbital period (687 days).

For example, a Periodogram analysis of the price data for Gold futures reveals dominant cycles of 420 days, 607 days, 740 days, and 760 days. In the context of planetary orbits and axial spins, these cycles are closely correlated as follows:

- 13 Mercury axial spins (762 days) are close to 760 days
- 3 Venus axial spins (729 days) is within a 1.5% margin of error to 740 days.
- 2 ½ Venus axial spins (607 days) align exactly to the 607-day cycle.
- 7 Mercury axial spins (411 days) are within a 2% margin of error to 420 days.

The key observation is that there is *not* one single planetary event that correlates to the dominant cycles that underpin price action of stocks, commodities, and indices. Our solar system truly is a resonant system.

# CHAPTER FOUR

## *Sunspots*

In the early-1800s, German scientist Heinrich Schwabe conducted observations of sunspot activity using a filtered telescope. He statistically showed that sunspot activity behaved in approximately an 11-year cycle. This finding has come to be called the *Schwabe Cycle.* Not long after, in 1859, Swiss scientist Wolff suggested this cycle was somehow influenced by Venus, Earth, Jupiter, and Saturn. However, he was unable to mathematically prove out his idea.

In 1919 American researcher George Hale concluded that the magnetic field behavior of the Sun followed an approximately 22-year cycle. He determined that the magnetic polarity of the Sun switches after each 11-year sunspot cycle. This finding has come to be called the *Hale Cycle*.

Since 1931, various researchers have pointed to Venus, Earth, and Jupiter as the primary cause of this solar cycle. In 1967, E.K. Bigg observed that when Mercury was at its closest approach to the

Sun (perihelion), it was capable of inducing an increase in solar flare activity. Although he could not explain it in detail, he suggested that this flare activity was amplified if another planet was on the same side of Sun as Mercury. Bigg's observations can be seen to have an effect on the financial markets. Consider the following examples:

Figure 4-1 has been annotated with Mercury perihelion events: March 2024 and June 2024.

At the March 18, 2024 perihelion event, Mercury made a 120-degree aspect to Venus as it approached perihelion. On the day of exact perihelion, it made a 90-degree square to Earth, and as it pulled away from perihelion it made a 120-degee aspect to Saturn. In response to the closeness of Mercury to the Sun and the aspects to other planets, the S&P 500 faded by 300 points. This overall perihelion event suggests that planets need not exclusively be on the same side of the Sun as Mercury to create an effect on solar flare emissions.

At the June 13, 2024 perihelion event, as Mercury approached perihelion, it recorded a 0-degree conjunction to Jupiter. On the day of exact perihelion, Mercury was nearly at a conjunction with Venus. The bullish trend in place (May 31 to July 16) was not disturbed at all by these planetary events. However, it is curiously interesting that the perihelion event came at the *geometric mean* of the bullish run. The geocentric mean of two numbers (such as a price high and low) is the square root of the multiplication product of the two numbers. Geocentric means are often found at key planetary events. The question of why remains unanswered. Perhaps one day this cosmic mystery will be understood.

**Figure 4-1**
Mercury Perihelion

Figure 4-2 has been annotated with three Mercury perihelion events: September 2024, December 2024, and March 2025.

At the left side of the chart, the Mercury perihelion event on September 6, 2024 was followed by a 500 point bullish move higher. This perihelion event had Jupiter a handful of degrees from Mercury (same side of Sun) which amplified gravitational inertia on the Sun.

At the December 6, 2024 perihelion event, the S&P 500 faded by 300 points. This event had Earth conjunct to Mercury (on the same side of the Sun). The gravitational effect on the Sun induced solar flare activity which weighed on human emotion.

At the March 4, 2025 perihelion event, the market was correcting already and the gravitational torque generated by Jupiter being conjunct to Mercury agitated negative emotion which propelled the selling to continue. This perihelion event is another example of the geocentric mean phenomenon occurring at a key planetary event.

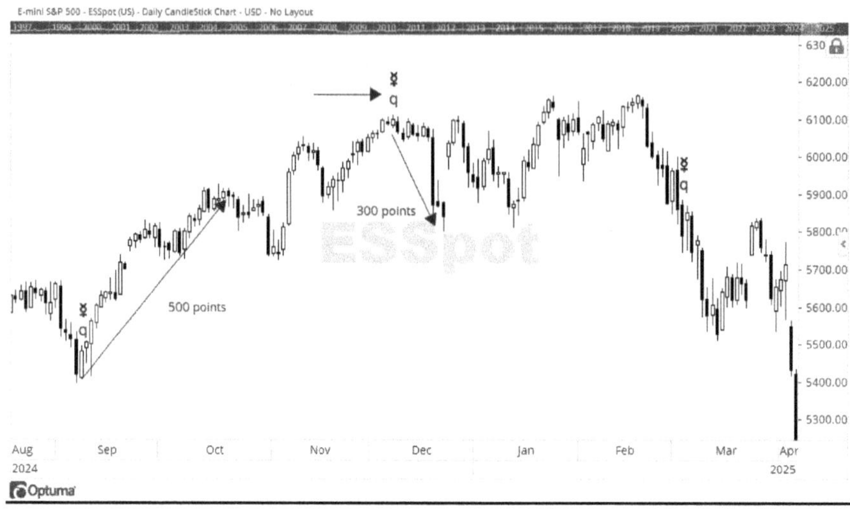


**Figure 4-2**
Mercury Perihelion

Mercury perihelion events affect more than just the equity market as the daily price chart of Gold futures in Figure 4-3 shows. The chart has been annotated with two perihelion events: May 2025 and August 2025.

At the perihelion event on May 30, 2025, only a modest move higher resulted. Earth and Venus were not in proximity to Mercury. Jupiter was a full 13-degrees away from Mercury.

A powerful rally in Gold price unfolded on the heels of the August 27, 2025 Mercury perihelion event which had Venus within a few degrees of being conjunct to Mercury.

The key observation from these two examples is to pay attention to all Mercury perihelion events, especially those with other planets located in close proximity to Mercury. Traders and investors should examine the heliocentric planetary placements a couple days before and after the exact perihelion event to see what planets might be in aspect to Mercury. As with all planetary events, perihelion events must be studied along with a chart trend technical indicator such as the Slow Stochastic.

**Figure 4-3**
Mercury Perihelion and Gold futures

## 2026 Perihelion Events

For 2026, Mercury perihelion events will occur as follows:

February 19, 2026: No other planets are in aspect to Mercury on the exact day of perihelion. However, the day after will have Mercury at 120-degree aspect to Venus.

May 18, 2026: Leading up to the exact perihelion event, Mercury will make a 60-degree aspect to Saturn. At exact perihelion, Mercury will be 60-degrees to Venus.

August 14, 2026: No other planets in close proximity to Mercury at perihelion. However, Earth is 120-degrees trine.

November 10, 2026: Leading up to the exact perihelion event, Mercury will make a 60-degree aspect to Saturn. Earth and Jupiter will be 90-degrees square to one another, and Jupiter and Saturn will be 120-degrees trine.

Planetary resonance studies have deepened the understanding of solar sun spot activity. In 2007, NASA researcher C.C. Hung showed that 25 of the 38 largest solar flares ever to have occurred started when one or more of Mercury, Venus, Earth, or Jupiter were either within 10 degrees longitude from the coronal emission flare site on the Sun's surface or were within 10 degrees of being opposite the flare site. His reasoning was that gravitational and inertial forces affected solar atmospheric pressures, the gravity field, and the magnetic field on the plasma layers of the Sun to create solar coronal emissions.

In 2012, Italian researcher Nicola Scafetta addressed the planetary amplification of solar flares in the context of the 22-year Hale Cycle. His work showed that gravitational and inertial forces created by Venus, Earth, Jupiter, and Saturn acting on the surface layers of the Sun amplified nuclear fusion and solar tidal activity by up to 4 million times. Scafetta further determined that gravitational forces associated with the orbital periods of Venus, Earth, and Jupiter combine to produce a 22.14-year cycle:

$$P(vej) = 1/[3/Pv - 5/Pe + 2/Pj] = 22.14; \text{ where}$$

Pv is the Venus heliocentric orbital period of 224.7 days, Pe is the Earth's heliocentric orbital period of 365.25 days, and Pj is Jupiter's heliocentric orbital period of 4332.58 days.

Scaffeta further determined that the data from the approximately 11-year Schwabe cycle, when analyzed using a Periodogram function, comprises four closely related cycles: 9.97 years, 10.66 years, 11.01 years, and 11.87 years. A 53.06 year cycle also exists, which is a 5$^{th}$ harmonic relation to the 10.66-year cycle (5 x 10.66 =53.30)

In 2013, Australian researcher Wilson extended Scafetta's work and showed that the torque forces created by the orbits of Venus and Earth serve to change the rotation rate of the Sun's surface layers in cycles of 11.07 years. His work further confirmed that the 11.07-year cycle is mathematically bounded by the ½-cycle of Jupiter and Saturn (9.93 years) and the Jupiter orbital period of 11.86 years. However, not all solar cycles are long in duration. The surface layers of the Sun also display short-term cyclical activity.

Swedish researcher Hans Jelbring has determined that there is a resonant relationship between planetary heliocentric orbits and the sunspot cycle. A total of 46 orbits of Mercury equal 11.079 years; 18 orbits of Venus equal 11.074 years; and 137 synodic Moon orbits (29.5 days) equal 11.077 years.

# CHAPTER FIVE

## *Sun and Moon Cycles*

In September, 1859, British astronomer Richard Carrington observed the largest solar flare in recorded history. Carrington was known for his solar research and had determined that the Sun was not a solid body, but rather a fluid-like plasma with various axial rotation rates. He observed that the part of the Sun at 26-degrees above its equatorial mid-point had an axial spin rate of 25.38 days. This phenomenon has since come to be called the *Carrington Cycle.*

In 2023, Scafetta and Wilson confirmed that 25.38 days is in fact the orbital spin time of the surface layers of the Sun at a distance of 26-degrees above the solar equator - a predominant area for coronal mass ejections.

Scafetta and Wilson further mathematically showed that from a vantage point on Earth (geocentric), there is a 24.7-day connection between the orbital period of Jupiter and the rotational spin time of the equatorial region of the Sun's surface. They also showed there to be a 26.5-day connection between the orbital period of Earth and the rotational spin time of the equatorial region of the Sun's surface. Lastly, they showed there to be 27.75-day connection between the axial spin rate of Venus and the rotational spin time of the equatorial region of the Sun's surface.

These shorter Sun cycles are not necessarily the only shorter cycles that affect human emotion and the financial markets. The closest orbiting body to Earth is the Moon. The Moon's orbit around the Earth can be described in terms of either synodic or sidereal cycles. The sidereal period of the Moon is 27.3 days (as viewed from a fixed reference like the Sun) and the synodic period is 29.5 days (as viewed from our vantage point here on Earth). This latter period lends itself to the expression lunar month. The gravitational pull of the Moon on planet Earth causes ocean tides to occur. As well, the gravitational pull of the Moon causes small shifts in the Earth's surface. Does this gravitational pull also affect human emotion?

Two less-frequently mentioned lunar cycle measures are the *draconitic month* and *the anomalistic month*. A draconitic month is the time for the Moon to go from being conjunct the North Node of Moon to once again being conjunct the North Node. On average, this timeframe is 27.2 days. An anomalistic month is the time of takes Moon to go from being at perigee (closest to Earth) to once again being at perigee, about 27.5 days.

When studying daily price charts from a short-cycle perspective, an expedient approach is to consider that the Sun cycles and Moon cycles are all in and around the 27-day range. A reasonable approach, then, is for one to apply a 27-day cycle interval to price charts.

Figure 5-1 shows a daily price chart of Mag-7 market darling NVIDIA (ticker NVDA) with 27-day cycles overlaid from a start point at the April 2025 sell-off lows. Dashed vertical lines denote the mid-point of the cycles. The lower pane on the chart is the 10/3 Slow Stochastic. A close study of the chart shows that the cycle endpoints and mid-points align to short term trend changes on the Stochastic plus or minus one day.

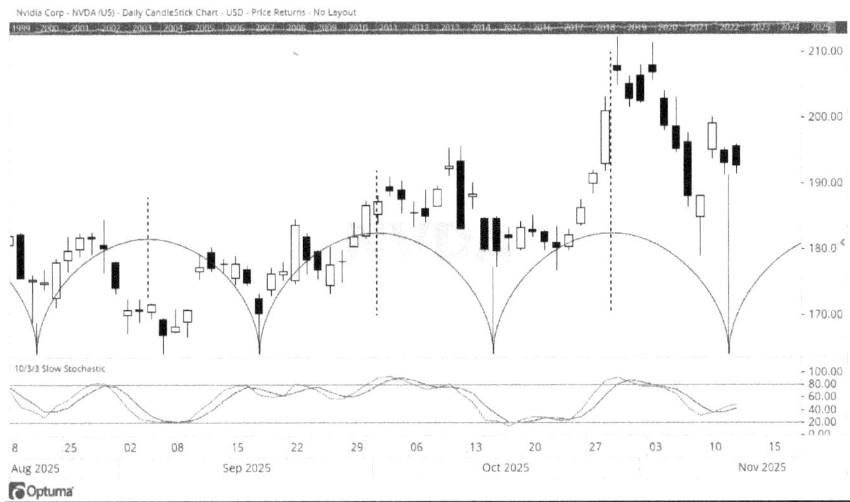


**Figure 5-1**
27-day cycles and Nvidia (NVDA)

As an interesting aside, not only do planets express resonance with one another, but so too do Moon and Earth. Swedish physicists Nordling and Österman have determined there is a resonance between the Earth and the Moon. Six Earth orbits equate to 2,190 days (365 x 6). They have calculated this is very close to the sidereal cycle between one draconitic and one anomalistic month (2,190.3 days).

To better appreciate short cycles in the context of the markets, consider the price charts of Silver futures and WTI Oil futures with cycles of 27-days overlaid. Figure 5-2 presents the daily chart of Silver futures prices. A close look of the chart shows that the cycle endpoints and mid-points align to short term trend changes on the Stochastic plus or minus one day.

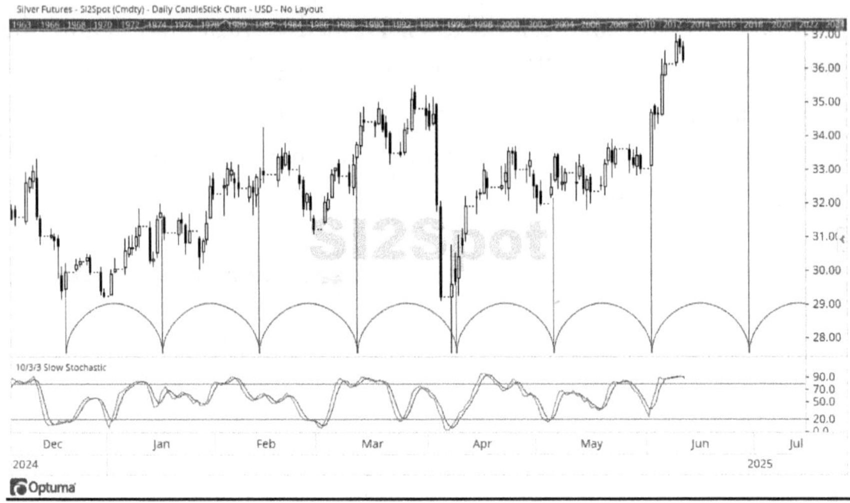


**Figure 5-2**
Silver and with a 27-day cycle

**Figure 5-3**
WTI Crude Oil with a 27-day cycle

Figure 5-3 is a daily chart of WTI Crude Oil prices with the 27-day cycle overlaid. A close study of the chart shows that the cycle endpoints and mid-points align to short term trend changes on the Stochastic plus or minus one day.

## Declination

Swedish researcher Jelbring takes the position that the declination changes in the Moon's orbital pattern around the Earth affect the angular momentum of the upper atmosphere wind currents which in turn affect weather patterns on Earth. Taking this one step further, one can imagine that human emotion is also affected by lunar declination. In the 1920's and 1930s, W.D. Gann was said to have paid attention to the declination of the Moon when making trading decisions. Jelbring's work now shows why lunar declination is important to follow.

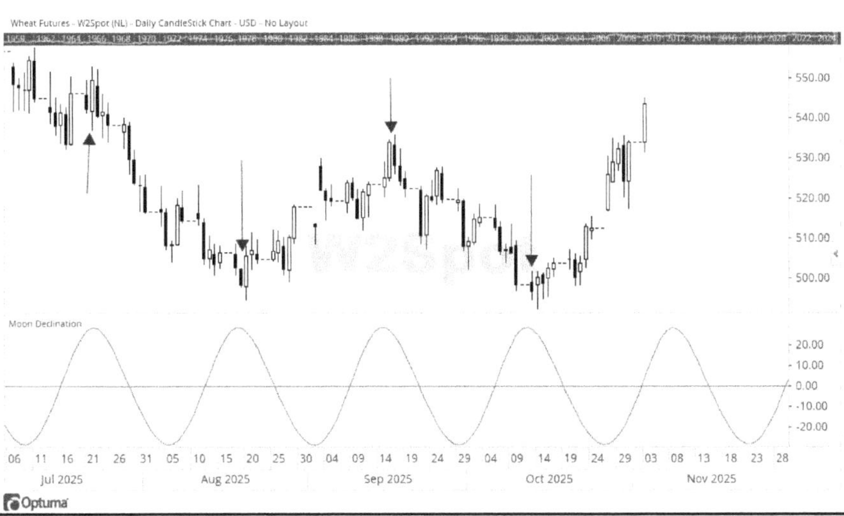


**Figure 5-4**
Wheat Futures and Lunar Declination

Figure 5-4 presents a daily chart of Wheat futures with lunar declination in the lower pane. The correlation between price swing points and declination extrema is obvious.

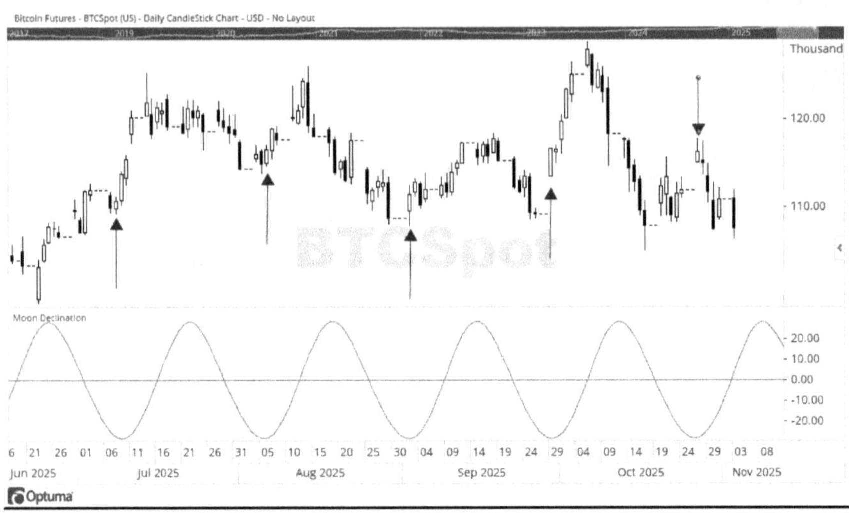


**Figure 5-5**
BitCoin Futures and Lunar Declination

Figure 5-5 presents a daily chart of BitCoin futures with lunar declination in the lower pane. The correlation between price swing points and declination extrema is obvious.

## 2026 Declination Dates

In 2026, Moon will be at its *declination maximum* on the following dates:

- January 2, January 30, February 26, March 25, April 21, May 19, June 15, July 13, August 9, September 5, October 2, October 30, November 26, December 24.

In 2026, Moon will be at its *declination minimum* on the following dates:

- January 16, February 13, March 12, April 8, May 5, June 2, June 29, July 26, August 22, September 19, October 16, November 12, December 10.

# CHAPTER SIX

## *Mercury Cycles*

In addition to cycles particularly related to sunspot activity and Mercury perihelion, there are other cycles that align to the orbital period of Mercury and the axial spin time of Mercury.

Mercury is the smallest planet in our solar system (about 3,000 miles in diameter) and the closest of all the planets to the Sun. As a result of its proximity to the powerful gravitational pull of the massive Sun, Mercury completes one orbit around the Sun in only 87.97 days (88 days in round figures) relative to a fixed point in space (heliocentric). The gravitational forces acting on Mercury also slow down its rate of axial spin; Mercury spins one time around its axis in 58.65 days.

### Mercury Torque

Not only does the Sun exert gravitational pull on Mercury, but Mercury imparts gravitational torque and inertia to the surface layers of the Sun. Mathematical determinations by Italian astronomer Nicola Scafetta have shown that Mercury's gravitational torque can be expressed by what he calls the Torque Index equation.

$$\text{Torque Index} = |\cos \theta \text{ ij}|$$

That is, it is the absolute value of the cosine of the angle subtended between heliocentric Mercury and another planet. In this equation, i and j denote the two planets (Mercury and either Venus, Earth, Jupiter, or Saturn) and θ denotes the heliocentric angle between them. When Mercury is at either 0-degrees or 180-degrees to the other planet, the conditions for maximum torque exist. This is because the absolute value of the cosine of either 0 or 180-degrees is equal to 1. When the two planets are at 90-degrees to one another, the conditions exist for minimum torque. This is because the absolute value of the cosine of 90 degrees is equal to 0. An angle of 120-degrees or an angle of 60-degrees provides for an intermediate level of torque as the absolute value of the cosine of 120 degrees or the cosine of 60 degrees is 0.5.

**Figure 6-1**
Gold futures and Mercury

For example, as Figure 6-1 illustrates, in August 2025 the price of Gold began a bullish advance from a sideways consolidation pattern. This bullish development was triggered by Mercury being 0-degrees conjunct to Venus (Torque Index =|cos θ ij |= 1.0).

Figure 6-1 also shows how Mercury alignments played a role in the price retraction of Gold in late October, 2025. At this price peak, Mercury was 120-degrees to Jupiter, 120-degrees to Venus, and 60-degrees to Saturn. The Torque Index equation for these pairs of aspects sums to 0.5+0.5+0.5 = 1.5.

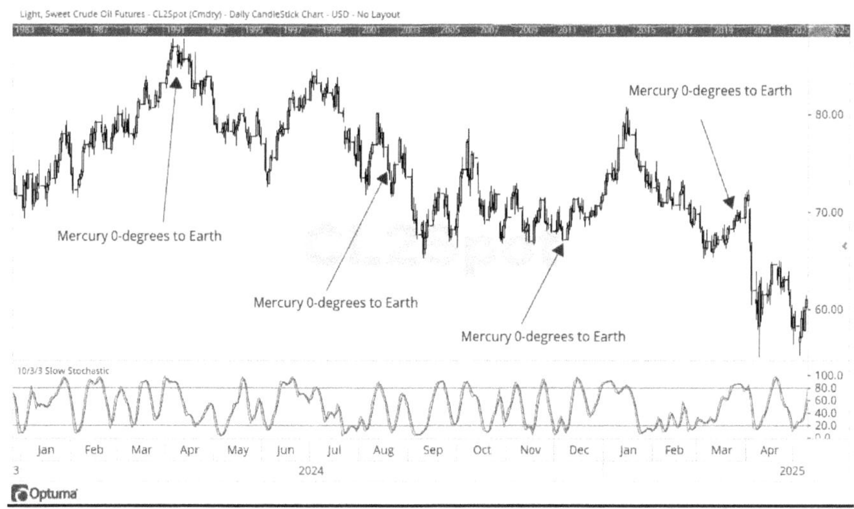


**Figure 6-2**
WTI Crude Oil and Mercury retrograde

There is one Mercury 0-degree aspect to be very mindful of and that is the heliocentric Mercury 0-degree conjunction to Earth. This is what classical, geocentric-focused astrologers refer to as Mercury retrograde. Traders and investors should watch price and trend action about four days on either side of the actual 0-degree conjunction event. Figure 6-2 illustrates price action on WTI Crude Oil futures at Mercury/Earth conjunction events in 2024 and into 2025. Note the alignment to price pivot points. These Mercury 0-degree events can be further made more volatile if other planets are also at an aspect to the conjunct pair.

## Mercury Aspects 2026

For 2026, Mercury will be at the following aspects which will influence the Torque Index equation:

| DATE | ASPECT(S) |
|---|---|
| January 1-2 | Mercury 120-degrees Saturn |
| January 10-12 | Mercury 90-degrees to Saturn |
| January 15-23 | Mercury 180-degrees to Earth,<br>Mercury 180-degrees to Jupiter,<br>Mercury 60-degrees to Saturn |
| January 24-27 | Mercury 0-degrees to Venus |

| DATE | ASPECT(S) |
|---|---|
| February 3-6 | Mercury 0-degrees to Saturn<br>Mercury 120-degrees to Jupiter |
| February 9-10 | Mercury 120-degrees to Earth<br>Mercury 90-degrees to Jupiter |
| February 15-16 | Mercury 90-degrees to Earth<br>Mercury 60-degrees to Jupiter |
| February 21-22 | Mercury 60-degrees to Earth |
| February 23-24, 2026 | Mercury 0-degrees to Jupiter |
| February 27-28, 2026 | Mercury 120-degrees to Venus |

| DATE | ASPECT(S) |
|---|---|
| March 6-9 | Mercury 0-degrees to Earth<br>Mercury 60-degrees to Jupiter |
| March 10-12 | Mercury 180-degrees to Saturn |
| March 16-18 | Mercury 90-degrees to Jupiter |

| | |
|---|---|
| March 22-29 | Mercury 180-degrees to Venus<br>Mercury 120-degrees to Jupiter |
| March 29-30 | Mercury 120-degrees to Saturn |
| February 27-28, 2026 | Mercury 120-degrees to Venus |

| DATE | ASPECT(S) |
|---|---|
| April 1-3 | Mercury 60-degrees to Earth |
| April 9-11 | Mercury 90-degrees to Saturn |
| April 17-20 | Mercury 180-degrees to Jupiter<br>Mercury 90-degrees to Earth<br>Mercury 60-degrees to Saturn |
| April 28-30 | Mercury 120-degrees to Earth |

| DATE | ASPECT(S) |
|---|---|
| May 1-6 | Mercury 120-degrees to Jupiter<br>Mercury 120-degrees to Venus<br>Mercury 0-degrees to Saturn |
| May 9-11 | Mercury 90-degrees to Jupiter<br>Mercury 90-degrees to Venus |
| May 14-16 | Mercury 180-degrees to Earth<br>Mercury 60-degrees to Jupiter and Saturn |
| May 17-18, 2026 | Mercury 60-degrees to Venus |
| May 20-21, 2026 | Mercury 90-degrees to Saturn |
| May 24-26 | Mercury 0-degrees to Jupiter<br>Mercury 120-degrees to Earth<br>Mercury 120-degrees to Saturn |

| DATE | ASPECT(S) |
|---|---|
| June 1-3 | Mercury 0-degrees to Venus<br>Mercury 90-degrees to Earth |
| June 8-9 | Mercury 180-degrees to Saturn |
| June 11-16 | Mercury 90-degrees to Jupiter<br>Mercury 60-degrees to Earth |
| June 25-27 | Mercury 120-degrees to Saturn<br>Mercury 120-degrees to Jupiter |

| DATE | ASPECT(S) |
|---|---|
| July 7-10, 2026 | Mercury 90-degrees to Saturn<br>Mercury 60-degrees to Venus |
| July 10-14, 2026 | Mercury 0-degrees to Earth |
| July 16-18 | Mercury 180-degrees to Jupiter<br>Mercury 60-degrees to Saturn |
| July 25-28 | Mercury 90-degrees to Venus |

| DATE | ASPECT(S) |
|---|---|
| August 1-2 | Mercury 0-degrees to Saturn<br>Mercury 120-degrees to Jupiter |
| August 5-6 | Mercury 120-degrees to Venus |
| August 7-8 | Mercury 90-degrees to Jupiter |
| August 12, 2026 | Mercury 60-degrees to Jupiter and Saturn |
| August 14-15 | Mercury 120-degrees to Earth |
| August 18-19 | Mercury 180-degrees to Venus<br>Mercury 90-degrees to Saturn |
| August 22-23 | Mercury 0-degrees to Jupiter<br>Mercury 120-degrees to Saturn |
| August 27-28 | Mercury 180-degrees to Earth |

| DATE | ASPECT(S) |
|---|---|
| October 5-7, 2026 | Mercury 90-degrees to Earth and Saturn |
| October 10, 2026 | Mercury 0-degrees to Saturn |
| October 13-17, 2026 | Mercury 60-degrees to Saturn<br>Mercury 180-degrees to Jupiter |
| October 16-19 | Mercury 60-degrees to Venus |
| October 19-21 | Mercury 60-degrees to Earth |
| October 29-31 | Mercury 0-degrees to Saturn |

| DATE | ASPECT(S) |
|---|---|
| November 3-7 | Mercury 0-degrees to Earth<br>Mercury 0-degrees to Venus<br>Mercury 90-degrees to Jupiter |
| November 9-10 | Mercury 60-degrees to Jupiter |
| November 14-15 | Mercury 60-degrees to Earth<br>Mercury 90-degrees to Saturn |

| | |
|---|---|
| November 18-21 | Mercury 0-degrees to Jupiter<br>Mercury 60-degrees to Venus<br>Mercury 90-degrees to Earth |
| November 30 | Mercury 120-degrees to Earth<br>Mercury 90-degrees to Venus |

| DATE | ASPECT(S) |
|---|---|
| December 1-4, 2026 | Mercury 120-degrees to Earth<br>Mercury 180-degrees to Saturn |
| December 14-18, 2026 | Mercury 120-degrees to Venus<br>Mercury 90-degrees to Jupiter |
| December 20-21, 2026 | Mercury 120-degrees to Venus |
| December 22-25, 2026 | Mercury 120-degrees to Jupiter and Saturn |
| December 29-30, 2026 | Mercury 180-degrees to Earth |

## Mercury Declination

The declination of Mercury above or below the ecliptic plane can also influence the gravitational torque forces that are imparted to the Sun.

For 2026, Mercury will be at its **declination maximum** around February 23, May 19, August 15, and November 18.

For 2026, Mercury will be at its **declination minimum** around January 15, April 12, July 10, and October 8.

## Mercury Orbit and Axial Spin Cycles

Periodogram analyses of various indices and commodity futures show that predominant price cycles are often multiples of Mercury's orbital period of 87.97 days (88 days in round figures) or its axial spin time of 58.65 days.

Figure 6-3 illustrates how the price of Gold futures reacted to these Mercury's cycles in 2025. From a swing point in late October 2024, 88-day cycles can be seen aligning very closely to other pivot points, including the price peak at near $4400 per ounce in October 2025. The 58.65-day cycles can also be seen aligning to pivot points. In fact, the 58.65-day cycle that terminated in late September aligned to the geometric mean of the bullish run that was in place at the time.

**Figure 6-3**
Gold futures and Mercury cycles

# CHAPTER SEVEN

## *Venus Cycles*

Venus is the second planet from the Sun and measures about 7,500 miles in diameter. It is sometimes referred to as Earth's twin, given that the diameter of Earth is just slightly larger at 7,900 miles.

Venus completes one orbit around the Sun in 225 days relative to a fixed point in space (heliocentric). Venus spins one time around its axis very slowly in 243 days.

### Venus Torque

Taking the work of Scafetta and applying it to Venus suggests that aspects of Venus to Mercury, Earth, Jupiter, or Saturn will yield gravitational torque forces on the Sun.

The equation Torque Index = $|\cos \theta\ ij|$ describes whether or not the angle between Venus and another planet will make for maximum gravitational torque. In this equation, i and j denote the two planets and $\theta$ denotes the heliocentric angle between them. The equation being contained in vertical bars means that the absolute value of the equation must be considered. When the two planets are at either 0-degrees or 180-degrees to one another, the conditions for maximum torque exist. This is because the absolute value of the cosine of either 0 or 180-degrees is equal to 1. When the two planets are at 90-degrees to one another, the conditions exist for minimum torque. This is because the absolute value of the cosine of 90 degrees is equal to 0. Angles of 60 or 120-degrees provide for an intermediate level of torque as the absolute value of the cosine of 120 or 60 degrees is 0.5.

**Figure 7-1**
Venus and Soybean Price

Figure 7-1 illustrates a daily price chart for Soybean futures. The chart has been annotated with aspects of Venus to other planets. As this example suggests, Venus aspects are a valuable tool to use to anticipate price pivot points and trend changes.

## Venus in 2026

For 2026, Venus will be at the following aspects which will create a response in the Torque Index equation:

| DATE | ASPECT(S) |
|---|---|
| January 1-10, 2026 | Venus 180-degrees to Earth |
| January 7-10, 2026 | Venus 180-degrees to Jupiter |
| January 14-18, 2026 | Venus 60-degrees to Saturn |
| January 24-27, 2026 | Venus 0-degrees to Mercury |
| February 16-20, 2026 | Venus 120-degrees to Jupiter |
| February 20-22, 2026 | Venus 90-degrees to Mercury<br>Venus 120-degrees to Jupiter |
| February 22-25, 2026 | Venus 0-degrees to Saturn<br>Venus 90-degrees to Mercury |
| February 27-28, 2026 | Venus 120-degrees to Mercury |
| March 9-11, 2026 | Venus 90-degrees to Jupiter |
| March 24-26, 2026 | Venus 180-degrees to Mercury |
| March 27-April 1, 2026 | Venus 60-degrees to Jupiter |

| DATE | ASPECT(S) |
|---|---|
| April 1-3, 2026 | Venus 60-degrees to Saturn |
| April 11-23, 2026 | Venus 120-degrees to Earth |
| April 19-24, 2026 | Venus 90-degrees to Saturn |
| May 1, 2026, | Mercury 120-degrees to Venus |
| May 5-10, 2026 | Venus 0-degrees to Jupiter |
| May 10, 2026 | Venus 90-degrees to Mercury |
| May 10-13, 2026 | Venus 120-degrees to Saturn |
| May 17-18, 2026 | Venus 60-degrees to Mercury |
| May 25-31, 2026 | Venus 90-degrees to Earth<br>Venus 0-degrees to Mercury |
| June 1-6, 2026 | Venus 90-degrees to Earth<br>Venus 0-degrees to Mercury |
| June 16-19, 2026 | Venus 180-degrees to Saturn |

| DATE | ASPECT(S) |
|---|---|
| July 2-7, 2026 | Venus 90-degrees to Jupiter |
| July 8-10, 2026 | Venus 60-degrees to Mercury |
| July 14-20,2026 | Venus 60-degrees to Earth |
| July 25-28, 2026 | Venus 90-degrees to Mercury<br>Venus 120-degrees to Saturn |
| August 5-7,2026 | Venus 120-degrees to Mercury |
| August 13-16, 2026 | Venus 90-degrees to Saturn |
| August 18-19, 2026 | Venus 180-degrees to Mercury |
| September 1-5, 2026 | Venus 180-degrees to Jupiter<br>Venus 60-degrees to Saturn |
| September 5-7, 2026 | Venus 120-degrees to Mercury |
| September 25-28, 2026 | Venus 90-degrees to Mercury |

| DATE | ASPECT(S) |
|---|---|
| October 10-12, 2026 | Venus 0-degrees to Saturn/Earth |
| October 11-13, 2026 | Venus 120-degrees to Jupiter |
| October 16-19, 2026 | Venus 60-degrees to Mercury |
| October 19-29, 2026 | Venus 0-degrees to Earth |
| October 30-31, 2026 | Venus 90-degrees to Jupiter |
| November 3-7, 2026 | Venus 0-degrees to Mercury<br>Venus 90-degrees to Jupiter |
| November 18-21, 2026 | Venus 60-degrees to Saturn/Jupiter |
| November 19-30, 2026 | Venus 90-degrees to Mercury |
| December 6-10, 2026 | Venus 90-degrees to Saturn |
| December 14-19, 2026 | Venus 120-degrees to Mercury |
| December 25-29,2026 | Venus 120-degrees to Saturn |
| December 27-31, 2026 | Venus 0-degrees to Jupiter |

## Venus Declination

The declination of Venus above or below the ecliptic plane can also influence the gravitational torque forces that are imparted to the Sun.

For 2026, Venus will be at its declination maximum around April 22 and again around November 30.

For 2026, Venus will be at its declination minimum around January 1, and again around August 10.

Figure 7-2 illustrates a daily chart of Soybean futures with Venus extreme declination events annotated on the chart. Note the alignment to price pivot points.

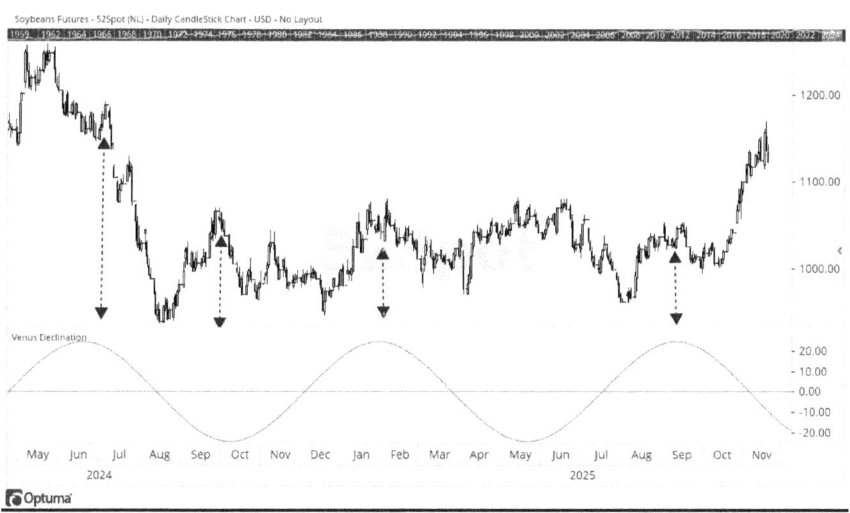


**Figure 7-2**
Venus declination and Soybean Price

## Venus Conjunctions

To a viewer situated on Earth (geocentric), there will be a period of time of about 50 days in duration when Venus is not visible to the naked eye. The reason is that it is *behind* the Sun which obscures its visibility. On a heliocentric zodiac wheel, this event will be seen as Venus and Earth making a 180-degree opposition to one another. This event is called the *Superior Conjunction* of Venus.

When Venus emerges from this 50-day span of obscurity, Venus will be visible in the early evening sky (the *Evening Star*) for the following 263 days. During this 263-day span, there will be a day when Venus is situated exactly between Earth and Sun. This is called the *Inferior Conjunction* of Venus. On a heliocentric zodiac wheel, Venus and Earth will appear 0-degrees conjunct to one another at Inferior Conjunction.

Following Inferior Conjunction, Venus will be visible in the early morning sky (the *Morning Star*).

**Figure 7-3**
Venus, Coffee prices, and Conjunctions

Figure 7-3 illustrates daily price activity for Coffee futures. The chart has been fitted with a 2024 Venus 180-degree opposition to Earth event (Superior Conjunction) and a 2025 Venus 0-degrees to Earth event (Inferior Conjunction).

The Superior Conjunction event in May 2024 marked the start of a gradually-rising bullish move that lasted for over 6 months. Leading up to the Earth-Venus opposition (Superior Conjunction), Jupiter was opposite to Earth. Mercury also posted a 120-degree aspect to Jupiter.

In mid-February 2025, Coffee prices recorded a reversal point triggered by Venus 120-degrees trine to Jupiter and Mercury 90-degrees square to Earth. The Inferior Conjunction event in March 2025 added to the weakness with a 15% decline.

## Conjunctions 2026

Heliocentric Venus will make a 0-degree aspect to Earth from October 19, 2026 through to October 29, 2026.

Heliocentric Venus will make a 180-degree aspect to Earth from January 1, 2026 through to January 11, 2026.

## Venus Orbit and Axial Spin Cycles

Periodogram analyses of various indices and commodity futures show that predominant price cycles are sometimes multiples of the Venus orbital period (225 days) or the Venus axial spin time of 243 days.

For example, Figure 7-4 illustrates how the price of Soybean futures reacted to the Venus orbital cycle from 2023 into 2025. At the far left of the chart, the 225-day cycle has been overlaid starting from a price swing pivot point in late May 2023. Note how the first cycle interval terminates in the middle of a bearish decline. This termination point is exactly at the geocentric mean of this bearish decline (mid-November 2023 to late February 2024). The next cyclic interval terminates at an important low in August 2024. The next cyclic interval terminates at a reversal point in April 2025. The current cyclical interval shown on the chart terminated in mid-November 2025. Note too how the mid-points of these cyclic intervals also align to price swing points.

**Figure 7-4**
Venus orbital cycles and Soybean futures

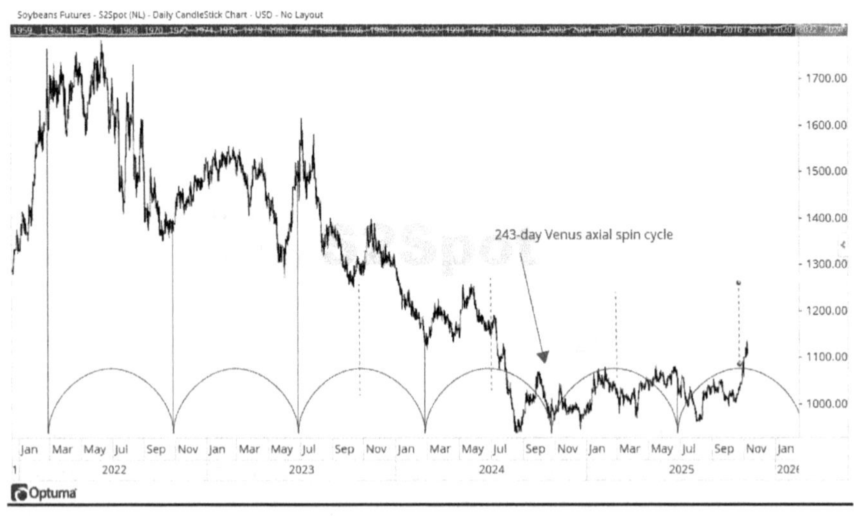


**Figure 7-5**
Venus axial spin cycles and Soybean futures

Figure 7-5 illustrates how the price of Soybean futures reacted to the 243-day Venus axial spin cycle from 2022 into 2025. At the far left of the chart, the 243-day cycle has been overlaid starting from a price swing pivot point in late February 2022. Note the following cycle end/start points:

- at a swing low in October 2022.
- at a swing high in July 2023.
- at a pivot point in February 2024.
- at a pivot point in October 2024.
- at a pivot point in June 2025.

The current cyclical interval shown on the chart will terminate in February 2026. Note too how the mid-points of these cyclic intervals also align to price swing points.

It is hard to predict exactly what price will do at the start or end points of these Venus cycle events. Traders and investors must be prepared for unusual volatility. This is where the use of a trend-following oscillator is essential.

Appendix 1 contains helpful information on price trends according to Gann and Gartley. In addition, Appendix 1 explains in detail how Oscillator functions can be used to discern the trend.

# CHAPTER EIGHT

## *Earth, Jupiter, and Saturn*

The equation for the Torque Index = $|\cos \theta \, ij|$ can be extended beyond just Mercury and Venus. It can be extended to examine pairings of three planets: Torque Index $= |\cos \theta \, ij| + |\cos \theta \, ik|$.

In this equation, i and j denote planets one and two; i and k denote planets one and three; θ denotes the heliocentric angle between the pairs of planets. The equation components being contained in vertical bars means that the absolute value of the components must be considered.

For example, if planets one and two were separated by 0-degrees and planet three was 180-degrees opposite to the pair, the above equation would compute to a value of 2.0 which indicates maximum torque conditions. If planets one and two were separated by 0-degrees and if planet three was 90-degrees from the pair, the torque equation would compute to a value of 1.0 which still presents strong torque conditions. Planet three at a 120-degree aspect to the conjunct pair would give a torque value of 1.5. Planets one, two, and three at 90-degree aspects to each another would give a torque value of 0 and would suggest minimal torque conditions.

Figure 8-1 shows a daily chart of Coffee futures prices. On January 17, 2024, Earth, Mercury, and Venus were all at aspect to one another and the Torque Index was at a value of 1.5. A few days later Saturn moved into a 120-degree aspect to both Mercury and Venus. This maintained the Torque Index equation at a value of 1.5. A swing pivot price pattern was the result.

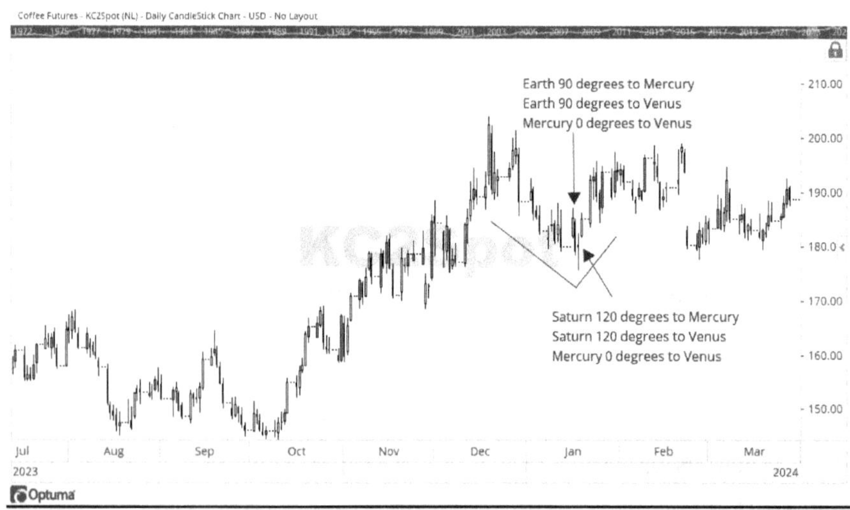


**Figure 8-1**
Coffee futures and multi-planet aspects

Figure 8-2 shows a daily chart of Gold futures prices. In mid-March, 2024 the multi-planet aspects spelled the end of what had been a bullish move higher. The subsequent sideways consolidation was brought to and end in late March at another multi-planet set of aspects.

**Figure 8-2**
Gold futures and multi-planet aspects

## Earth, Jupiter, Saturn in 2026

For 2026, the following aspects involving Earth, Jupiter, and Saturn.

| DATE | ASPECT(S) |
|---|---|
| January 6-14, 2026 | Earth 0-degrees to Jupiter |
| January 16-25, 2026 | Earth 120-degrees to Saturn |

| DATE | ASPECT(S) |
|---|---|
| March 13-17, 2026 | Jupiter 60-degrees to Earth |
| March 27-April 1, 2026 | Venus 60-degrees to Jupiter |

| DATE | ASPECT(S) |
|---|---|
| April 13-22, 2026 | Earth 90-degrees to Jupiter |
| May 17-29, 2026 | Jupiter 120-degrees to Earth<br>Earth 120-degrees to Saturn |

| DATE | ASPECT(S) |
|---|---|
| June 17 – year end | Saturn 120-degrees to Jupiter |
| June 25-July 3, 2026 | Earth 90-degrees to Saturn |

| DATE | ASPECT(S) |
|---|---|
| July 25-30, 2026 | Earth 180-degrees to Jupiter |

| DATE | ASPECT(S) |
|---|---|
| August 1-2, 2026 | Earth 180-degrees to Jupiter<br>Earth 60-degrees to Saturn<br>Earth 60-degrees to Mercury |

| DATE | ASPECT(S) |
|---|---|
| October 1-7, 2026 | Earth 0-degrees to Saturn |
| October 29-31, 2026 | Venus 90-degrees to Jupiter |

| DATE | ASPECT(S) |
|---|---|
| November 3-9, 2026 | Earth 90-degrees to Jupiter |
| December 2-8, 2026 | Earth 60-degrees to Saturn |
| December 5-13, 2026 | Earth 60-degrees to Jupiter |

# CHAPTER NINE

## *Equity and Commodity Cycles*

### S&P 500

Applying the Periodogram function to the daily price chart of the S&P 500 futures reveals several dominant cycles: 446 days, 495 days, 520 days, and 602 days. These cycles closely align to:

- 2 orbits of Venus around the Sun (450 days) which is very close to 446 days
- 2 axial spins of Venus about its axis (486 days) which is very close to 495 days
- 6 orbits of Mercury around the Sun (528 days) which is very close to 520 days
- 2 ½ axial spins of Venus about its axis (607 days) which is very close to 602 days.

The daily price chart in Figure 9-1 has been fitted with a Venus 243-day cycle starting from the market high that was developing in late 2021. The chart has also been fitted with a 225-day cycle starting from a swing low point in October 2021.

Note how the 243-day cycle matched the low in August 2024 and also the low in April 2025. The most recent 243-day cycle pattern terminated December 12, 2025. If this 243-day cycle continues, traders and investors should watch the mid-August 2026 timeframe for the cycle to end again.

Note how the mid-point of the 225-day cycle aligned to a pivot point immediately ahead of the April 2025 sell-off. If the 225-day cycle continues, traders and investors should watch the late January 2026 and early September 2026 timeframes for the cycle to end again.

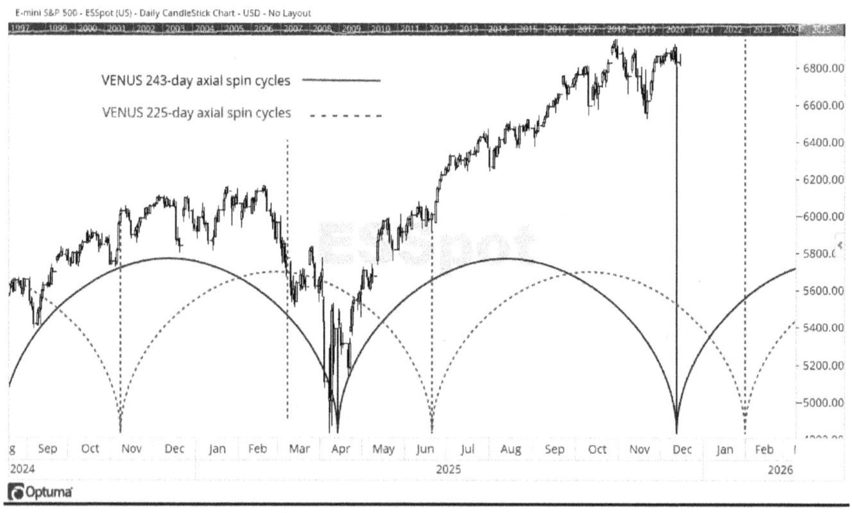


**Figure 9-1**
S&P 500 and Venus 243-day and 225-day cycles

The daily price chart in Figure 9-2 has been fitted with a Mercury 88-day cycle starting from the pivot point interim high that preceded the April 2025 sell-off. At the right side of the chart, the end of an 88-day increment aligned to the market's emotional response to news that the 2025 U.S. government shutdown would be ending. This shutdown, which was steeped in a quagmire of concerns over health care premium tax deductibility, was the longest shutdown in U.S. history.

From November 12, 2025, traders and investors should count forward in 88-calendar-day increments to identify the cycles in 2026.

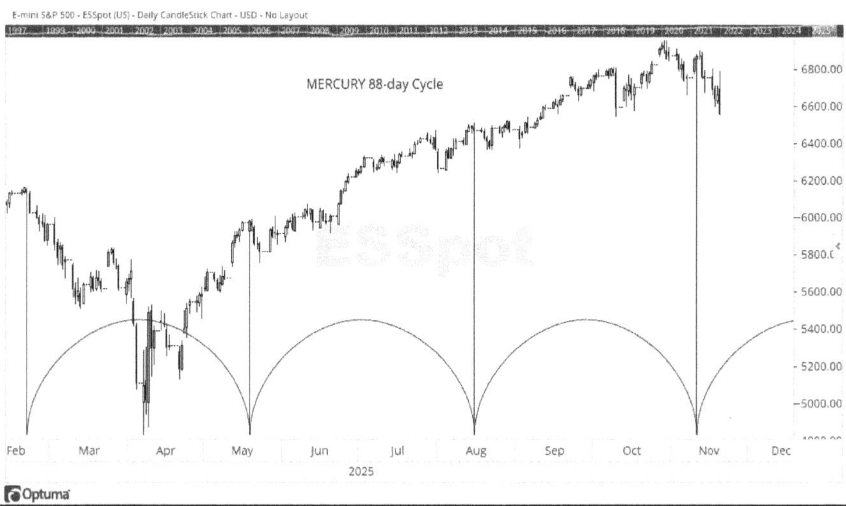


**Figure 9-2**
S&P 500 and Mercury 88-day cycle

# Nasdaq 100 Index

Applying the Periodogram function to the daily price chart of the Nasdaq 100 futures reveals dominant cycles 446 and 502 days. These align to:

- 5 orbits of Mercury around the Sun (440 days) which is very close to 446 days.
- 2 orbits of Venus around the Sun (450 days) which is very close to 446 days.
- 8 ½ axial spins of Mercury about its axis (499 days) which is very close to 502 days.

The daily price chart in Figure 9-3 has been fitted with a Venus 225-day cycle and a Mercury 88-day cycle. At the right side of the chart note how the midpoint of the Mercury cycle aligns to a failed counter-trend rally attempt.

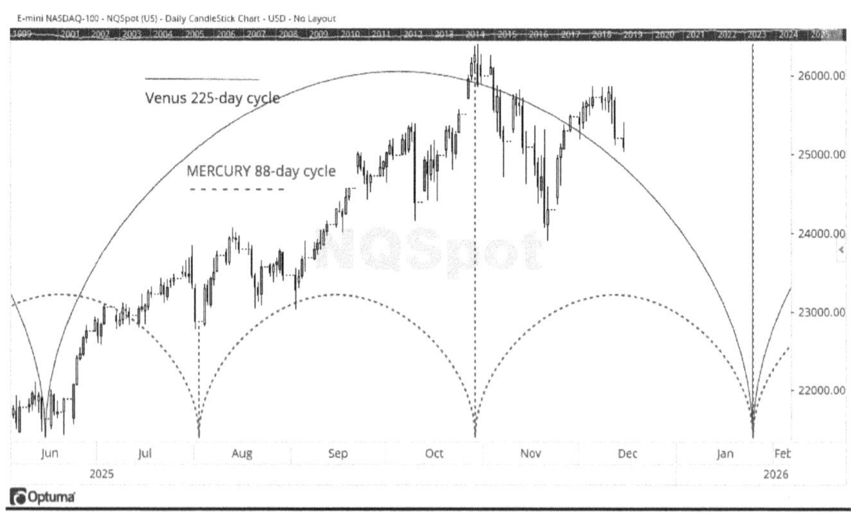


**Figure 9-3**
Nasdaq with Venus and Mercury cycles

If the 225-day cycle continues, traders and investors should watch the early September 2026 timeframe for the cycle to end again. From about January 25, 2026 adding increments of 88-calendar-days will identify the Mercury cycle end points during 2026. Remember to configure the price chart so that it shows calendar days and not just Monday through Friday price bars.

# Russell 2000 Small Cap Index

Applying the Periodogram function to the daily price chart of the Russell 2000 futures reveals dominant cycles 223 and 361 days. These align to:

- 1 orbit of Venus around the Sun (225 days) which is very close to 223 days.
- 1 orbit of Earth around the Sun (365 days) which is very close to 361 days.

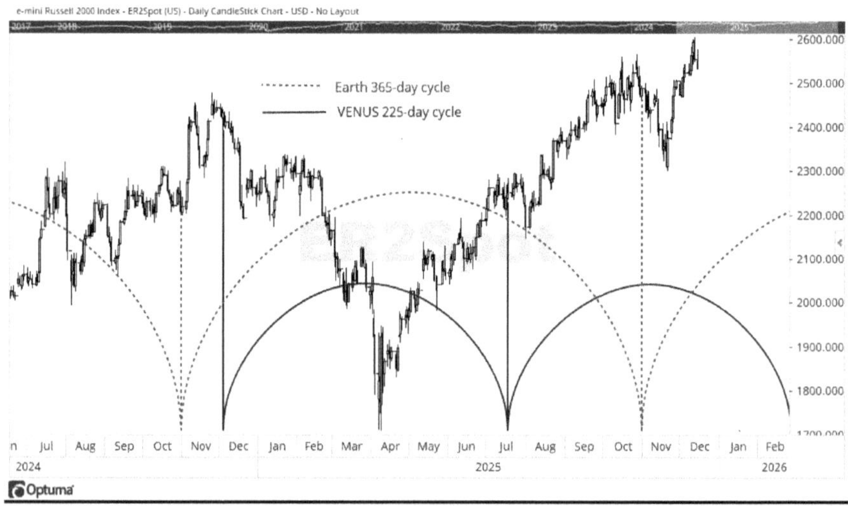


**Figure 9-4**
Russell 2000 with Earth and Venus cycles

The daily price chart in Figure 9-4 has been fitted with a Venus 225-day cycle and an Earth 365-day cycle. Note how the Earth cycle aligns to a swing high reversal point in early-November, 2025. If these cycles continue, traders and investors should watch for the Earth cycle to end in late October 2026. The Venus cycle could end in late February 2026 and again in mid-October 2026.

**Figure 9-5**
Russell 2000 with 27-day cycles

As suggested in an earlier chapter, the various Sun axial spin cycles can generally be combined with lunar cycles in the form of a 27-day cycle. The price chart in Figure 9-5 has been fitted with the Slow Stochastic indicator along with 27-day cycles. As suggested by cross-over events on the Stochastic indicator, cycle mid-points and end-points on the chart align closely to price inflection points. From early-December 2025, traders and investors can count forward in 27-day increments to gain insight into when these shorter cycles will manifest in 2026.

# Gold

The history of Gold revolves around several dates: the London Gold Fix creation date, the COMEX founding date, and the Gold futures first trade date.

Investors who follow daily Gold prices may not realize that working behind the scenes to define the daily price of Gold is an archaic methodology called the *London Gold Fix.* The London Gold Fix dates to September 12th, 1919 when the Bank of England made arrangements with N.M. Rothschild & Sons for the formation of a Gold-market in which there would be one official price for Gold bullion quoted on any one day. At 11:00 a.m., the first Gold fixing took place with the five principal Gold-bullion traders and refiners of the day present. These traders and refiners were: N.M. Rothschild & Sons, Mocatta & Goldsmidt, Pixley & Abell, Samuel Montagu & Co., and Sharps Wilkins.

In the geocentric horoscope for September 12, 1919, Sun, Mercury, Venus, and Saturn are all in the sign of Virgo, a not-so-subtle reference to the female goddess Isis who is associated with wisdom, foresight, and knowledge. Ancient Babylonian and Sumerian civilizations revered the planet Venus for its dual nature (visible as the Morning Star and also as the Evening Star). Ancient Egyptians further enhanced Isis by connecting her to the Osiris story. During the Roman era, Isis became connected to Venus - the Roman goddess of love, beauty, fertility, and magic. As classical, geocentric astrology gained a following in the 18th century, the zodiac sign of Venus took on these historical facets. It does not require a large stretch of the imagination to think that first trade dates in the world of finance are associated where possible with Venus.

Moreover, in the September 12th, 1919 heliocentric horoscope wheel, Earth and Venus are exactly conjunct. This is a suggestion that Gold might follow the 225-day heliocentric Venus cycle; a suggestion too that Gold might react to Venus retrograde events. In addition, at the time of the first price fixing in 1919, Mercury was at its maximum latitude and Venus was at its minimum latitude. The choice of September 12, 1919 to start the Gold Fix program was not a random selection.

Today, the London Gold Fix occurs at 10:30 a.m. and 3:00 p.m. local time each business day in London. Participants in the daily fixes are: Barclay's, HSBC, Scotia Mocatta (a division of Scotia Bank of Canada), and Societe Generale. These twice-daily collaborations (some would say collusions) provide a benchmark price that is then used around the globe to settle and mark-to-market the value of all the various Gold-related derivative contracts in existence.

The Commodity Exchange was started July 5, 1933 with the merger of the National Metal Exchange, the Rubber Exchange, the Raw Silk Exchange, and the Raw Hide Exchange. This newly formed exchange brought Gold trading to the U.S. for the first time. This exchange evolved over the following years to become COMEX. Today, the CME Group owns COMEX where Gold, Silver, Copper, Platinum, and Palladium futures instruments all trade.

July 5, 1933 was not a randomly chosen date. On this date, geocentric Sun was at 13 of Cancer which is within one degree of the geocentric Ascendant point on May 17, 1792 when the NYSE was founded. This date also had Mars and Jupiter in the sign of Virgo – another reference to Isis. Moreover, on July 5, 1933, Moon was at its minimum declination and Venus was at its maximum latitude.

In 1971, U.S. President Nixon eliminated the convertibility of Gold bullion into U.S. Dollars. This created the need for a futures pricing mechanism for Gold. A Gold futures contract was launched on December 31, 1974. If it seems odd that a futures contract would be launched on the final day of the calendar year when many traders would be off enjoying the Holiday season, consider that on this date Mercury and Venus were at their declination minima. Mercury was 180-degrees opposite Saturn (in the 1919 Gold Fix geocentric horoscope these two are 0-degrees conjunct). Mercury and Venus are within a handful of degrees of being conjunct, which is the same as in the 1933 COMEX horoscope wheel. The choice of December 31, 1974 was this not a random selection.

Applying the Periodogram function to the daily price chart of Gold futures reveals several dominant cycles: 760, 740, 607, and 420 days. These align to:

- 13 Mercury axial spins (762 days) which is close to 760 days.
- 3 Venus axial spins (729 days) which is within a 1.5% margin of error to 740 days.
- 2 ½ Venus axial spins (607 days) align exactly to the 607-day cycle.
- 7 Mercury axial spins (411 days) which is within a 2% margin of error to 420 days.

The daily Gold price chart in Figure 9-6 has been fitted with axial spin cycles of Venus and Mercury. A Mercury cycle aligned to the October 2025 significant price high. However, the mid-point of the Venus cycle also made the same alignment. This underscores the connectivity and resonance of the solar system. From the October 2025 high, traders and investors can count forward in increments of 58.65 days to determine when the Mercury axial spin cycles will land. The Venus cycle will end around mid-February 2026 and again in mid-October, 2026.

Applying a 27-day cycle to Gold prices reveals a very good alignment to price pivot points. The price chart in Figure 9-7 has been fitted with the Slow Stochastic indicator along with 27-day cycles. As suggested by cross-over events on the Stochastic, swing points on the chart align to cycle mid-points and end-points.

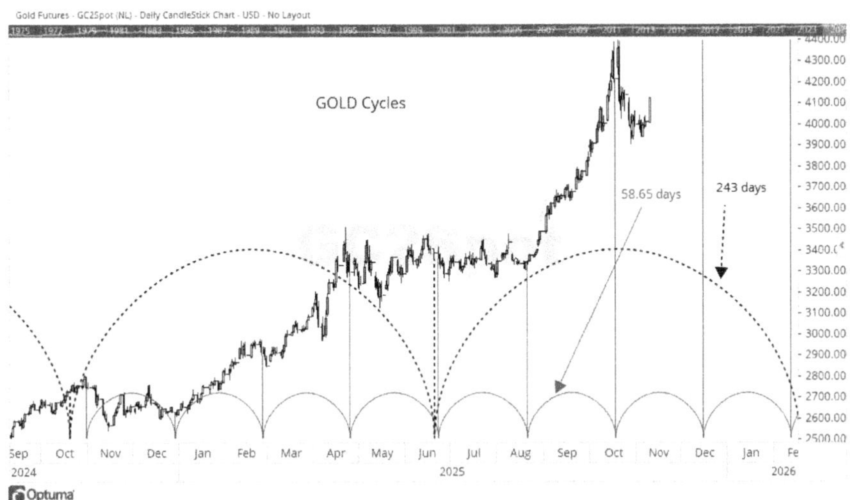


**Figure 9-6**
Gold with Mercury and Venus axial spin cycles

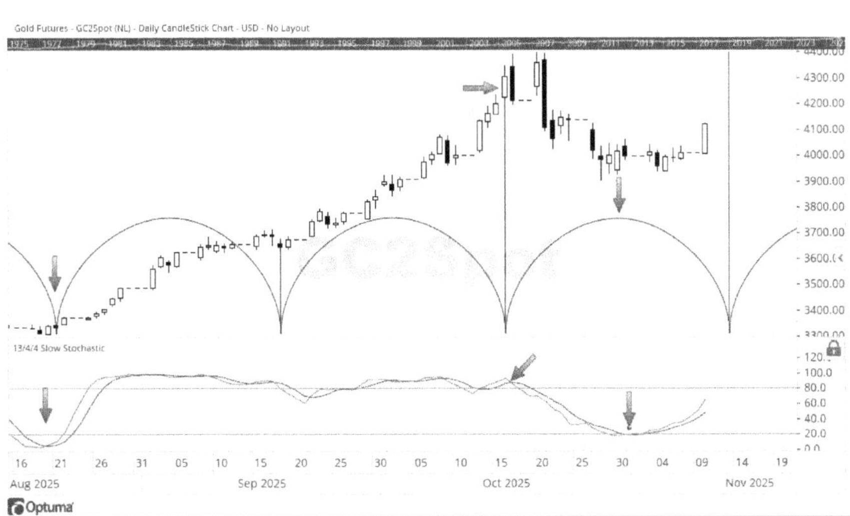


**Figure 9-7**
Gold price and 27-day cycles

# Silver

Silver futures started trading on COMEX on July 5, 1933 – the very date that COMEX officially became operational.

Applying the Periodogram function to the daily price chart of Silver futures reveals dominant cycles of 541 and 683 days. These align to:

- 9 ¼ Mercury axial spins (542 days) which is nearly exact to the 541-day cycle.
- 2 ¼ Venus axial spins (546 days) which is very close to the 541-day cycle.
- 1 Mars orbit around the Sun (687 days) which is very close to the 683-day cycle.
- 3 Venus orbits around the Sun (675 days) which is within a 1% margin of error to 683 days.

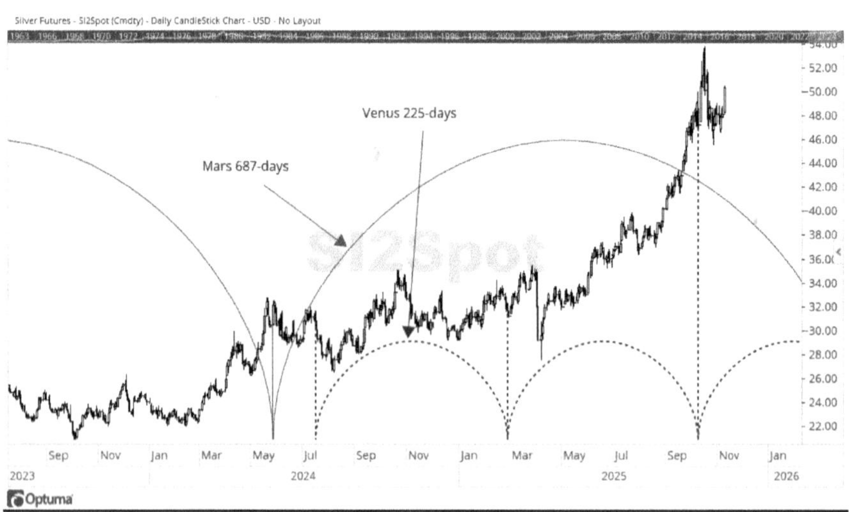


**Figure 9-8**
Silver price with Mars and Venus cycles

Figure 9-8 illustrates a Silver futures daily chart fitted with Mars and Venus orbital cycles. The mid-point of the Mars cycle aligns very closely to the April 2025 price retreat. A Venus cycle aligns to the October price highs.

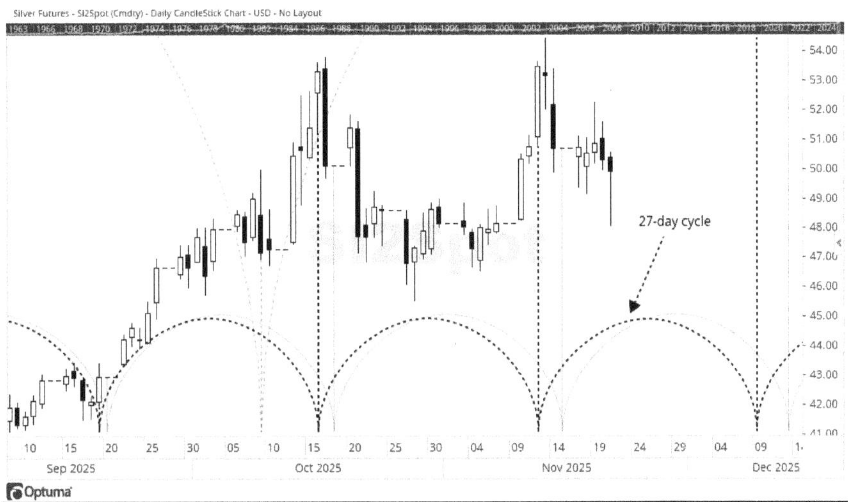


**Figure 9-9**
Silver price with a 27-day cycle

The current Mars cycle will end in mid-April 2026. The Venus cycle will end in late May 2026 and again in early January 2027.

Applying a 27-day cycle to Gold prices reveals a very good alignment to price pivot points. As the daily price chart in Figure 9-9 shows, a 27-day cycle aligns to the price swing high in mid-October, 2025 and to a similar swing pivot point on November 13, 2025. Traders and investors seeking to follow the 27-day cycle can count forward in 27-day increments from November 13.

# Copper

The first trade date for Copper futures was July 29, 1988. This date was a Full Moon. Sun and Mercury were conjunct. Moreover, Moon had just recorded its declination minimum, and Mercury was at its maximum declination.

Applying the Periodogram function to the daily price chart of Copper futures reveals several dominant cycles: 581,618, 676, and 703 days. These align to:

- 10 Mercury axial spins (586 days) is very close to the 581-day cycle.
- 7 Mercury orbits around the Sun (616 days) is very close to the 618-day cycle.
- 3 Venus orbits around the Sun (675 days) match the 676-day cycle.
- 12 Mercury axial spins (704 days) match the 703-day cycle.
- 8 Mercury orbits around the Sun (704 days) matches the 703-day cycle.

As the daily Copper price chart in Figure 10-10 shows, Copper prices align very well to the Venus 225-day cycle and also to the mid-point of the cycle. The end-point of the recently-concluded Venus cycle aligns to the April 2025 price lows. The mid-point of the cycle aligns to the sharp sell-off in late July 2025 when news that refined copper products would not be subject to any new tariffs. This news caught traders off-guard and prices fell in response. Traders and investors should watch the early-July 2026 timeframe for the next Venus cycle to end.

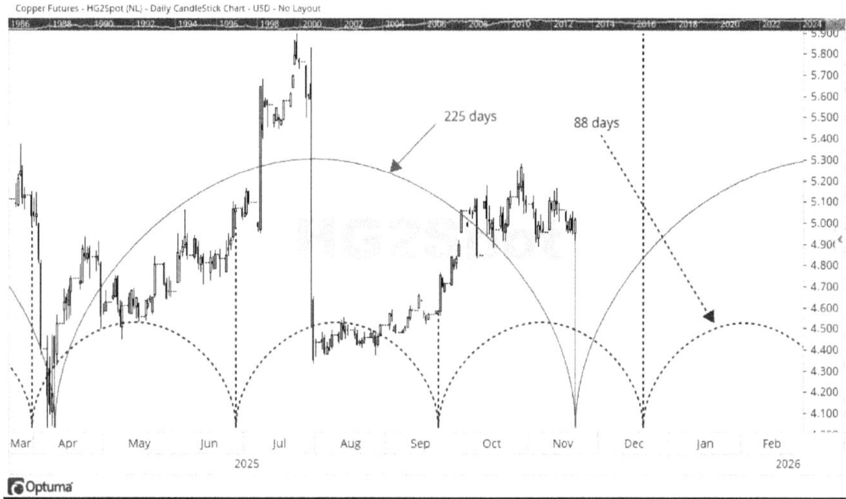


**Figure 9-10**
Copper futures with Venus and Mercury cycles

Copper prices also align well to the Mercury orbital period of 88-days. From December 20, 2025 traders and investors can project forward in 88-day increments to identify coming cycles. Although not shown on the chart, Copper prices also align well to the Mercury axial spin period of 58.65 days. From October 30, 2025 traders and investors can project forward in 58.65-day increments to identify coming cycles

# Platinum

Platinum futures started trading on COMEX in New York at 8:30 a.m. on December 3, 1956 with Moon at the Ascendant and Jupiter in Virgo (a reference to Isis). Mercury was at its declination minimum and latitude minimum and Venus was at its latitude maximum. The choice of December 3, 1956 as a first trade date was not a random selection.

Applying the Periodogram function to the daily price chart of Platinum futures reveals several dominant cycles: 529, 592, 616 days. These align to:

- 6 Mercury orbits around the Sun (528 days) matches the 529-day cycle.
- 10 Mercury axial spins (586 days) which is within is within a 1% margin of error to 592 days.
- 7 Mercury orbits around the Sun (616 days) exactly matches the 616-day cycle.

Traders and investors who follow Platinum price action can apply the Mercury orbital cycle by projecting forward in 88-day increments starting from October 17, 2025. The Mercury axial spin cycle can be applied by projecting forward in 58.65-day increments form November 25, 2025.

## Palladium

Palladium futures started trading in New York at 8:00 a.m. on January 22, 1968. Jupiter, Pluto, and Uranus were all the sign of Virgo (an Isis reference). On this date, Moon had just passed through 0-degrees declination and Mercury was at 0-degrees declination. The choice of this date to launch this futures contract was not a random selection.

Applying the Periodogram function to the daily price chart of Platinum futures reveals a dominant cycle of 616 days. A total of 7 Mercury orbits around the Sun (616 days) exactly matches this cycle. Traders and investors who follow Palladium price action can apply the Mercury orbital cycle by projecting forward in 88-day increments starting from around January 10, 2026.

# Canadian Dollar and British Pound

The Chicago Mercantile Exchange traces its roots to January 5, 1898 and the founding of the Chicago Butter and Egg Board. On December 1, 1919 the Board changed its name to the Chicago Mercantile Exchange when it received its clearing house license. On this date, Moon was passing through 0-degrees declination, Venus was at maximum latitude, Mercury was at 0-degrees latitude, and Venus was at maximum declination.

Canadian Dollar and British pound futures contracts both started trading on May 16th, 1972 on the Chicago Mercantile Exchange. On this date, the Ascendant was at 15 of Cancer – a close match to the Ascendant position at the founding date of the NYSE. Moon was at its maximum declination and Venus was at its maximum latitude. The choice of this date was not a random one.

Applying the Periodogram function to the daily price chart of Canadian Dollar futures reveals several dominant cycles: 769, 723, 608, and 595 days. These align to:

- 13 Mercury axial spins (763 days) which is very close to the 769-day cycle.
- 8 ¼ Mercury orbits around the Sun (726 days) very nearly matches the 723-day cycle.
- 2.5 Venus axial spins (608 days) exactly match the 608-day cycle.
- 6.75 Mercury orbits around the Sun (594 days) matches the 595-day cycle.

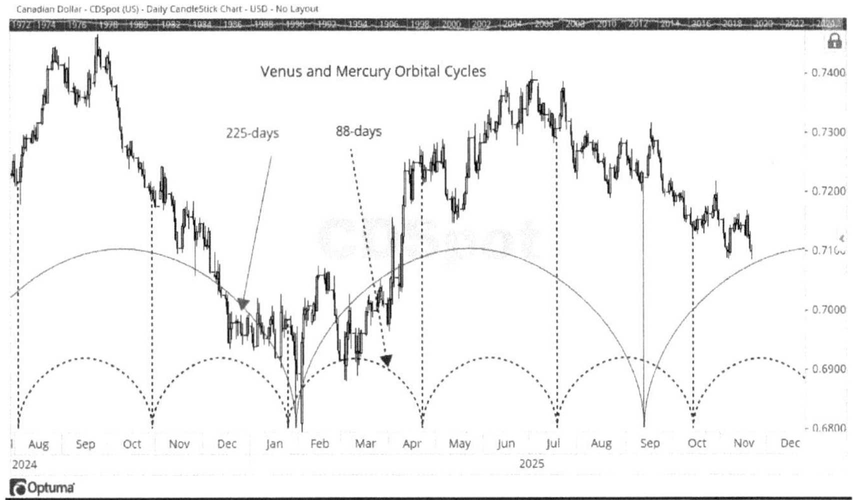


**Figure 9-11**
Canadian Dollar with Mercury and Venus cycles

Figure 9-11 illustrates a Canadian dollar futures daily chart fitted with Mercury and Venus orbital cycles. The mid-points of the Mercury cycles align very well to price pivot points. From mid-October 2025, traders and investors can project forward in 88-day increments to identify coming Mercury orbital cycles.

The current Venus 225-day cycle will terminate around late April 2026. The next Venus cycle will terminate in late December 2026.

Applying the Periodogram function to the daily price chart of British Pound futures reveals dominant cycles of 581 and 618 days. These align to:

- 10 Mercury axial spins (586 days) which is well within a 1% margin of error of the 581-day cycle.
- 7 Mercury orbits around the Sun (616 days) which very closely match the 618-day cycle.

**Figure 9-12**
British Pound with Mercury axial spin cycles and 27-day cycles

Figure 9-12 shows a daily price chart of British Pound futures fitted with a Mercury 58.65-day cycle and a Mercury 88-day cycle. From a start point around January 1, 2026, traders and investors can project forward in 58.65-day increments to identify coming Mercury axial spin cycles. Projections of 88-day increments from January 10, 2026 will identify coming Mercury orbital cycles.

# Euro Currency

The Euro became the official currency for the European Union on January 1, 2002 when Euro bank notes became freely and widely circulated. However, futures contracts had already started trading on the Chicago Mercantile Exchange on January 4, 1999. On this date, Moon was at its declination maximum and Mercury was at 0-degrees latitude. In the geocentric zodiac, Mercury, Saturn, and the North Node formed a perfect grand trine pattern (all 120-degrees from one another).

Applying the Periodogram function to the daily price chart of Euro Currency futures reveals several dominant cycles: 631, 598, and 561 days. These align to:

- 10 ¾ Mercury axial spins (630 days) which is a match to the 631-day cycle.
- 6 ¾ Mercury orbits around the Sun (594 days) which is a very close match to the 598-day cycle.
- 9 ½ Mercury axial spins (557 days) which is a very close match to the 561-day cycle.
- 2 ½ Venus axial spins (608 days) which is within a 1.5% margin of error to the 598-day cycle.

Figure 9-13 illustrates a Euro Currency futures daily chart fitted with Mercury and Venus cycles. From around December 24, 2025, traders and investors can project forward in 58.65-day increments to identify coming Mercury axial spin cycles. From mid-December, projections of 88-day intervals will show coming Mercury orbital cycles. From late December 2025, a forward projection of 243-days suggests the next Venus cycle will end in late August 2026.

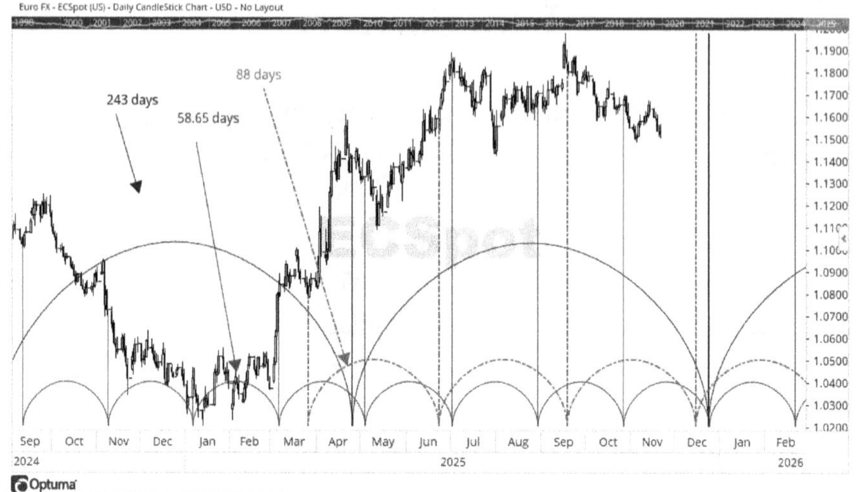


**Figure 9-13**
Euro Currency with Mercury and Venus cycles

## Australian Dollar

Australian dollar futures started trading on the Chicago Mercantile Exchange on January 13, 1987. On this date, geocentric Mercury and Sun were 0-degrees conjunct. On a heliocentric zodiac wheel, Venus was in Virgo (an Isis reference). Moon was at its declination maximum, Mercury was at its declination minimum, Venus was at maximum latitude, and Mercury was at minimum latitude.

Applying the Periodogram function to the daily price chart of Australian Dollar futures reveals several dominant cycles: 559, 593, and 691 days. These align to:

- 2.5 Venus orbits around the Sun (562 days) which closely aligns to the 559-day cycle.
- 10 Mercury axial spins (586 days) which is within a 1% margin of error of the 593-day cycle.
- 11 ¾ Mercury axial spins (689 days) which very closely aligns to the 691-day cycle.

Figure 9-14 illustrates an Australian futures daily chart fitted with Mercury and Venus cycles. From mid-February, 2026 traders and investors can project forward in 225-day increments to identify coming Venus orbital cycles. From around January 1, 2026 forward projections of 58.65-day increments will identify coming Mercury axial spin cycles.

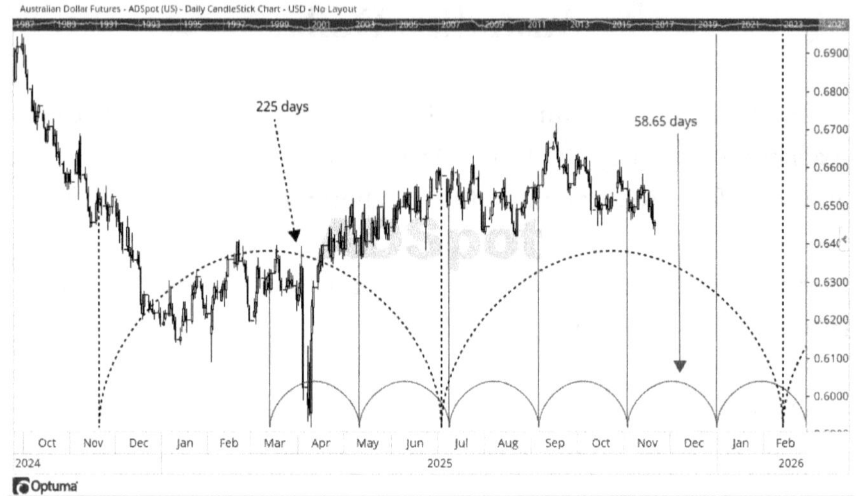


**Figure 9-14**
Australian Dollar futures with Mercury and Venus cycles

## Live Cattle

Live Cattle futures started trading on the Chicago Mercantile Exchange on November 30, 1964. Assuming a first transaction time of 7:00 a.m., Sun was at the Ascendant. In the heliocentric zodiac wheel, Venus was in Virgo and Mercury was 180-degrees opposite to Venus. In the geocentric zodiac, Venus, Saturn, and the North Node form a grand trine pattern with each planet 120-degrees from the others. Mercury was at its minimum latitude, Venus was at its maximum latitude, and Moon was at 0-degrees declination. It is highly unlikely that the choice of this date to launch a futures contract was a random pick.

Applying the Periodogram function to the daily price chart of Live Cattle futures reveals the dominant 362-day cycle is closely related to:

- One 365-day orbit of the Earth around the Sun.
- 6 ¼ axial spins of Mercury (366 days).

Figure 9-15 illustrates Live Cattle futures daily price action. The 365-day Earth cycle has been fitted to the chart along with the Mercury 58.65-day axial spin cycle, and a 27-day cycle.

From around December 21, 2025 traders and investors can project forward in 58.65-day increments to identify coming Mercury cycles. Early May 2026 will mark the start of a new 365-day Earth cycle.

**Figure 9-15**

Live Cattle futures with Earth, Mercury, and 27-day cycles

Figure 9-15 also shows that a 27-day cycle provides a reasonably good match to price pivot points. Traders can project forward from mid-December 2025 to start identifying coming cycles.

## Feeder Cattle

Feeder Cattle futures started trading on the Chicago Mercantile Exchange on November 30, 1971. Assuming a first transaction time of 7:00 a.m., Sun was at the Ascendant (the same location as in the Live Cattle geocentric wheel). On a geocentric zodiac wheel, Sun and Saturn are 180-degrees opposite; Mercury and Venus are 0-degrees conjunct. Pluto, North Node, and Saturn form a grand trine pattern. Moon was at 0-degrees declination and both Mercury and Venus were at 0-degrees declination.

Applying the Periodogram function to the daily price chart of Live Cattle futures reveals the dominant 361-day cycle is closely related to:

- One 365-day orbit of the Earth around the Sun.
- 6 ¼ axial spins of Mercury (366 days).

Figure 9-16 illustrates Feeder Cattle futures daily price action. Traders can watch the early May timeframe in 2026 for the end of the current Earth 365-day cycle. From late-November 2025, traders can project forward in 58.65-day increments to identify coming Mercury axial spin cycles. From the mid-October 2025 price peak, traders with a short-term focus can project forward with 27-day cycles.

**Figure 9-16**
Feeder Cattle futures with Earth, Mercury, and 27-day cycles

# Lean Hogs

Lean Hog futures started trading on the Chicago Mercantile on February 28, 1966. Venus was near 0-degrees declination, Moon was nearly at its declination maximum, and Mercury was at 0-degrees latitude.

Applying the Periodogram function to the daily price chart of Lean Hogs futures reveals several dominant cycles: 364, 564, 653 days. These align to:

- One orbit of Earth around the Sun (365 days) which matches the 364 day cycle.
- 2 ½ Venus orbits(562 days) around the Sun which matches the 564-day cycle.
- 7 ½ Mercury orbits around the Sun (660 days) which is within a 1% margin of error of the 653-day cycle.
- 11 Mercury axial spins (645 days) which is within a 1% margin of error of the 653-day cycle.

Figure 9-17 illustrates Lean Hogs futures daily price action. Traders can watch the mid-August timeframe in 2026 for the end of the current Earth 365-day cycle. From around November 8, 2025 traders can project forward with 88-day increments to identify coming Mercury orbital cycles. From mid-December 2025, traders can project forward with 58.65-day increments to identify coming Mercury axial spin cycles. From mid-October 2025, traders can project forward with 225-day increments to identify coming Venus orbital cycles.

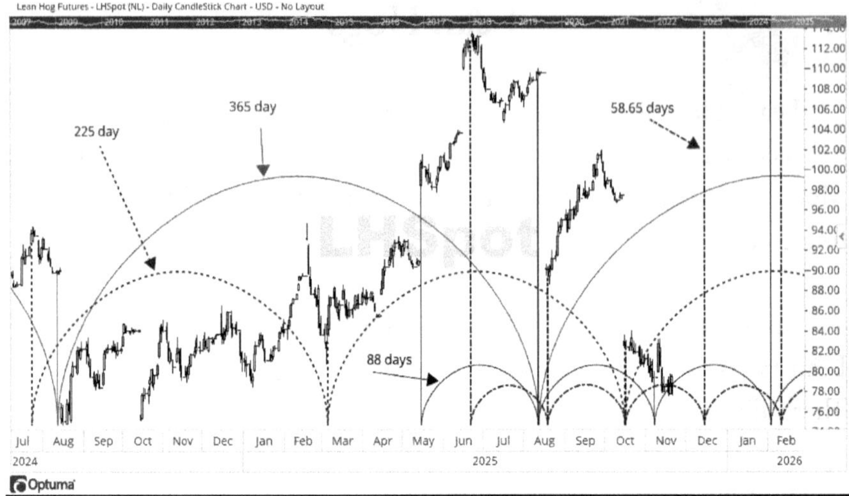


**Figure 9-17**
Lean Hogs futures with Earth, Venus, and Mercury cycles

# BITCOIN

A relatively recent addition to the trading lineup on the Chicago Mercantile Exchange is BitCoin futures.

Applying the Periodogram function to the daily price chart of Bitcoin futures reveals several dominant cycles: 196, 287, and 353 days These align to:

- 2 ¼ Mercury orbits around the Sun (198 days) which is a close match to the 196-day cycle.
- 5 Mercury axial spins (293 days) which is a close match to the 287-day cycle.
- 6 Mercury axial spins (352 days) which is a near-exact match to the 353-day cycle.

The Bitcoin price chart in Figure 9-18 has been fitted with Mercury cycles. There seem to be two Mercury orbital cycles with a phase offset of about 3 weeks. Note how a Mercury cycle aligns to the early October 2025 swing high at $128,500 per coin. Note how the offsetting Mercury cycle aligns to the lows made around November 21, 2025.

Traders can project forward in 58.65-day increments from November 20 and also from December 4, 2025 to identify coming Mercury cyclic events. must also pay attention to the mid-points of these various cycles. In early November, 2025 the mid-point of an 88-day Mercury orbital cycle lined up with the tipping point that sent BitCoin tumbling from the $107,0000 level. Traders can project forward from around December 22, 2025 to identify coming Mercury orbital cycles.

**Figure 9-18**
BitCoin futures with Mercury cycles

## Chicago Board of Trade

The Chicago Board of Trade started operations on April 3, 1848. On this date, Mercury and Venus were 0-degrees conjunct on the geocentric zodiac wheel. In addition, this date marked a New Moon event with Moon at 0-degrees declination. Initially the exchange focused on grains futures contracts. However, as time went on, a variety of new contracts were added - including Bond futures. Today, the Chicago Board of Trade is part of the CME Group empire.

## 30-Year Bond Futures

30-Year Bond futures started trading on the Chicago Board of Trade on August 22, 1977. Assuming an 8:20 a.m. first trade time, the Mid-Heaven was at 23 Gemini. In the CBOT horoscope, the Ascendant was at 23 Gemini. The choice of this date to launch this futures contract was not a random selection. At this first trade time, Both Mercury and the Ascendant were in the sign of Virgo (a reference to the goddess Isis). In addition, Mercury was at minimum declination and Moon was at its minimum declination also.

Applying the Periodogram function to the daily price chart of 30-Year Bond futures reveals several dominant cycles: 692, 795, and 854 days. These align to:

- 1 Mars orbit around the Sun (687 days) which is well within a 1% margin of error to the 692-day cycle.
- 9 Mercury orbits around the Sun (792 days) which is a match to the 795-day cycle.
- 1 ¼ Mars orbits around the Sun (859 days) which is a very close match to the 854-day cycle.

- 3 ½ Venus axial spins (850 days) closely match the 854-day cycle.

**Figure 9-19**
30-Year Bond futures with Mars and Venus cycles

The daily chart of 30-Year Bond futures in Figure 9-19 has been fitted with Mars orbital cycles and Venus axial spin cycles. The most recent Mars cycle terminated at November 10, 2025. The current cycle will terminate in early-October 2027. Late-October 2026 will see the mid-point of this Mars cycle.

Traders following the 30-Year Bond futures market can project forward in 243-day increments from November 1, 2025. The current Venus cycle will terminate in very-early July 2026. Thereafter, early November 2026 will mark a cycle mid-point.

# 10-Year Treasury Note Futures

10-Year Treasury Notes started trading in Chicago on May 3, 1982. Assuming an 8:20 a.m. first trade time, the Ascendant was at 23 Gemini – a match to the CBOT natal Ascendant. The selection of this date to launch this futures contract was not a random selection. In addition, on this date, Venus was at its minimum declination, Moon was at 0-degrees declination, and Mercury was at its maximum latitude.

Applying the Periodogram function to the daily price chart of 10-Year Treasury Note futures reveals several dominant cycles: 260, 507, and 687 days. These align to:

- 3 Mercury orbits around the Sun (264 days) which closely matches the 260-day cycle.
- 2 ¼ Venus orbits around the Sun (506 days) which closely match the 507-day cycle.
- 11 ¾ Mercury axial spins( 689 days) which closely match the 687-day cycle.

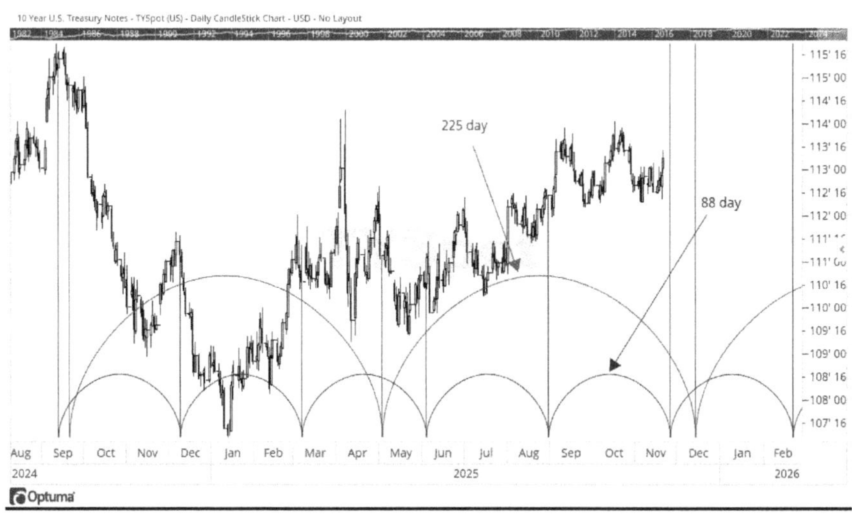


**Figure 9-20**

10-Year Treasury Note futures with Venus and Mercury cycles

The daily chart of 10-Year Treasury futures in Figure 9-20 has been fitted with Venus axial spin cycles and Mercury orbital cycles. The most recent Venus cycle ended in mid-December 2025. Traders who follow the 10-Year Treasury market can project forward in 225-day intervals to determine the next Venus cycle end-point (late July 2026). The Mercury orbital cycle can be projected forward in 88-day increments from around November 2025 to determine the next Mercury orbital cycles.

Figure 9-21 shows that a 27-day cycle provides a reasonably good match to price pivot points. Traders with a short time frame focus can project forward from around December 17, 2025 to start identifying future cyclic intervals.

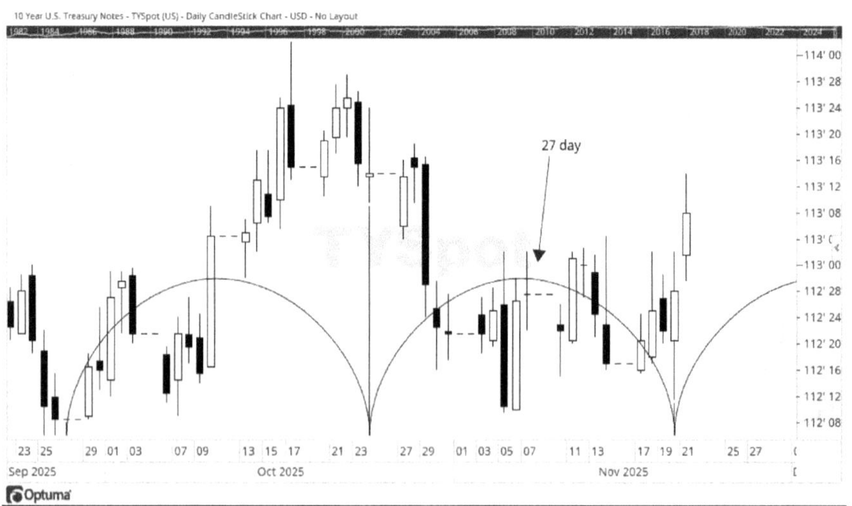


**Figure 9-21**
0-Year Treasury Note futures with 27-day cycles

# Wheat and Corn

Wheat and Corn futures all share the same first trade date of January 2, 1877. Assuming a 7:30 a.m. first trade time, geocentric Venus is 90-degrees square to the Venus Sun location in the 1848 CBOT natal horoscope. Moreover, Sun in the 1877 horoscope is 90-degrees square to the Sun in the 1848 CBOT horoscope. This choice of this date to launch these futures contracts was no accident. As well, on January 2, 1877 Moon was at its maximum declination.

Applying the Periodogram function to the daily price chart of Wheat futures reveals a few dominant cycles: 365, 540, and 548 days. These align to:

- One orbit of the Earth around the Sun (365 days) which is a perfect match to the 365-day cycle.
- 9 ¼ axial spins of Mercury (542 days) which is a close match to the 540-day cycle.
- 2 ¼ Venus axial spins (547 days) which is nearly exact to the 548-day cycle.

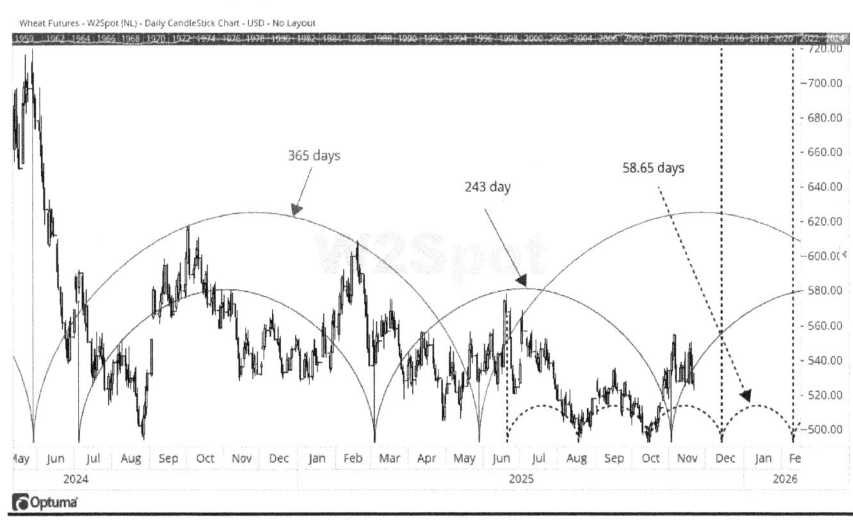


**Figure 9-22**
Wheat futures with Earth, Mercury, and Venus cycles

The daily Wheat price chart in Figure 9-22 has been fitted with Earth orbital cycles, Mercury axial spin cycles, and Venus axial spin cycles.

From mid-December 2025, traders can project forward in 58.65-day increments to determine future Mercury axial spin cycles. Late May 2026 will mark the start of a new Earth orbital cycle. From November 1, 2025 traders can project forward in 243-day increments to identify coming Venus axial spin cycles.

Applying the Periodogram function to the daily price chart of Corn futures reveals a few dominant cycles: 364, 504, 512, and 526 days. These align to:

- One Earth orbit around the Sun (365 days) which is a match to the 364-day cycle.
- 5 ¾ Mercury orbits around the Sun (506 days) which is a very close match to the 504-day cycle.
- 8 ¾ Mercury axial spins (513 days) which is a near exact match to the 512-day cycle.
- 6 Mercury orbits around the Sun (528 days) which is a very close match to the 526-day cycle.

The daily Corn futures price chart in Figure 9-23 has been fitted with an Earth cycle, Mercury orbital cycles and Mercury axial spin cycles.

Late February 2026 will mark the start of a new Earth cycle. Traders can project forward in 88-day increments from early November 2025 to identify future Mercury orbital cycles. Projecting forward in 58.65 day intervals from about December 20, 2025 will point to Mercury axial spin cycles in 2026.

**Figure 9-23**
Corn futures with Mercury cycles

# Soybeans

Soybean futures started trading in Chicago on October 5, 1936. In the geocentric horoscope, Sun is 180-degrees opposite to the position of the Sun in the CBOT 1848 horoscope. In the CBOT 1848 horoscope, Jupiter and Saturn were at a 120-degree aspect. In the Soybeans 1936 horoscope, Jupiter and Saturn are 90-degrees square. Assuming a 6:00 a.m. first trade time, the Mid Heaven in the 1936 Soybeans geocentric horoscope is at 14 Cancer, the same location as the Ascendant in the NYSE natal horoscope. In addition, Moon was at its declination maximum on this date. Venus was at its declination minimum. The choice of this date to launch the Soybeans contract was carefully calculated.

Applying the Periodogram function to the daily price chart of Soybeans futures reveals several dominant cycles: 364, 511, 629, and 709 days. These align to:

- One Earth orbit around the Sun (365 days) is a match to the 364-day cycle.
- 8 ¾ Mercury axial spins (513 days) is a near exact match to the 511-day cycle.
- 10 ¾ Mercury axial spins (630 days) is a near match to the 629-day cycle.
- 12 Mercury axial spins (703 days) is within a 1% margin of error to the 709-day cycle.

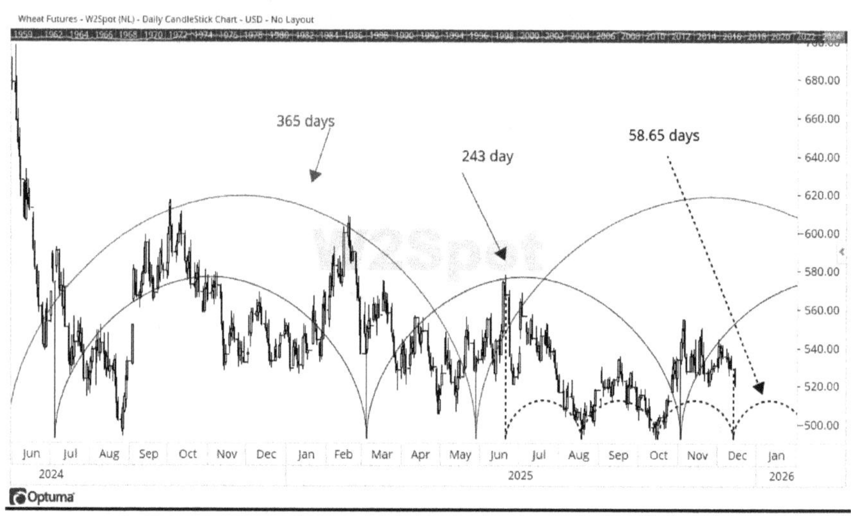


**Figure 9-24**
Soybean futures with Mercury cycles

The daily Soybean futures price chart in Figure 9-24 has been fitted with the Earth cycle as well as Mercury axial spin cycles. Soybean traders can project forward from late November 2025 in 58.65-day intervals to identify points of interest in 2026. October 2026 will mark the start of a new Earth cycle.

# The New York Cotton Exchange

In 1870, the controlling exchange for the global Cotton trade was located in Liverpool, U.K. In early 1870, a group of cotton merchants and brokers doing business in New York decided to create a Cotton Trading Association that would rival Liverpool by promoting a focus on fair dealing and fair pricing. By late 1870, the operational framework had been created and on April 8, 1871 the New York Cotton Exchange was granted a charter from the State of New York legislature. On this date, Moon was at its declination minimum. Assuming a 9:00 a.m. first trade time, geocentric Jupiter was on the Ascendant.

Applying the Periodogram function to the daily price chart of Cotton futures reveals two dominant cycles: 363 and 655 days. days. These align to:

- One Earth orbit around the Sun (365 days) which is a match to the 363-day cycle.
- 7 ½ Mercury orbits around the Sun (660 days) which is a close match to the 655-day cycle.

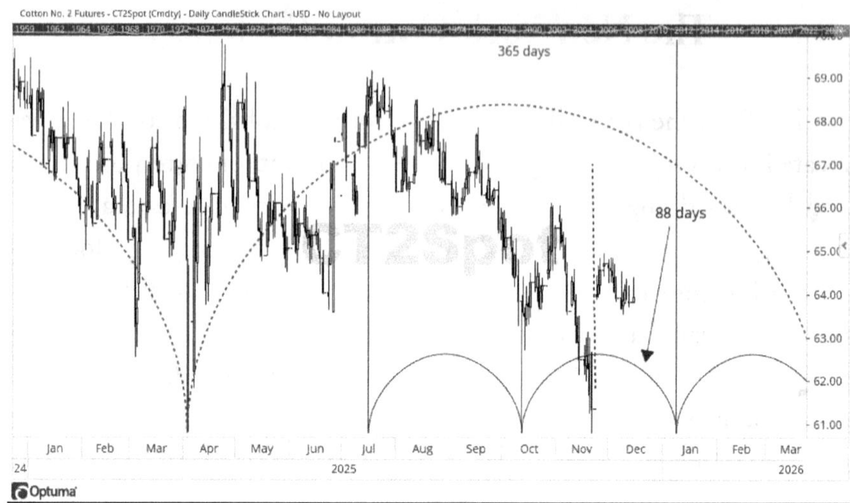


**Figure 9-25**
Cotton futures with an Earth and Mercury cycles

The daily Cotton futures price chart in Figure 9-25 has been fitted with the Earth cycle as well as Mercury orbital cycles. Note how the midpoint of the current 88-day cycle aligned to a wild price reaction; a spike low followed by a gap higher. Cotton traders can project forward from around January 8, 2026 in 88-day increments to identify points of interest in 2026. Early April 2026 will mark the start of a new Earth cycle.

## The New York Mercantile Exchange

In 1872 a group of merchants in New York created the Butter and Cheese Exchange. By 1882, opportunities to add new contracts to its trading floor beckoned. On April 25, 1882 the exchange was renamed the New York Mercantile Exchange. Despite a thorough internet search, an exact start date for 1872 could not be identified.

What is for sure though is that West Texas Intermediate (WTI) Crude Oil futures started trading for the first time on the New York Mercantile on March 30, 1983. Moon was at 0-degrees declination on this date. Mercury was at its minimum declination and at 0-degrees latitude.

Applying the Periodogram function to the daily price chart of Crude Oil futures reveals a few dominant cycles: 523, 628, and 706 days. These align to:

- 6 Mercury orbits around the Sun (528 days) which is a close match to the 523-day cycle.
- 10 ¾ Mercury axial spins (630 days) which is a very close match to the 628-day cycle.
- 8 Mercury orbits around the Sun (704 days) which is a very close match to the 706-day cycle.

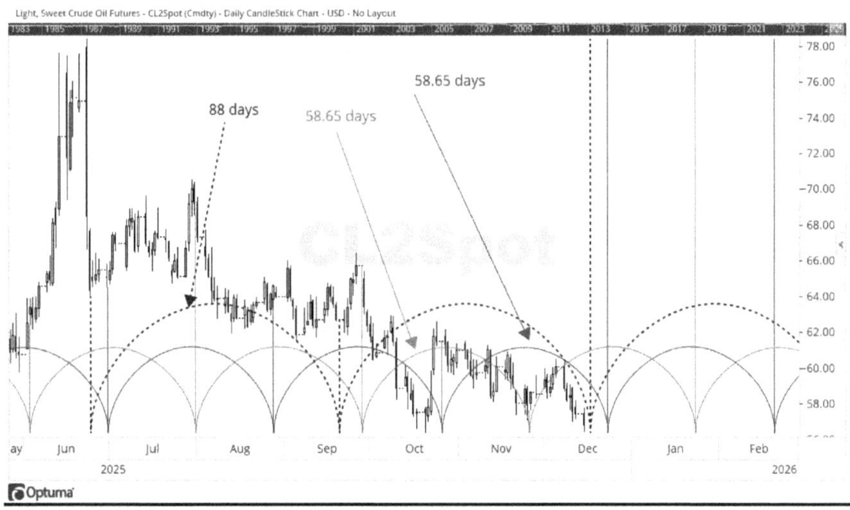


**Figure 9-26**
Crude Oil futures with Mercury cycles

The daily price chart in Figure 9-26 has been fitted with Mercury axial spin cycles and Mercury orbital cycles. There are two axial spin cycles which are approximately one-half cycle out of phase.

Traders and investors can project forward by 88-day increments from around December 17, 2025 to identify points of interest in 2026. For the Mercury axial spin cycles, projecting forward in 58.65-day increments from both November 26, 2025 and December 23, 2025 will identify points of interest in 2026.

## Natural Gas

Natural Gas futures started trading on the New York Mercantile Exchange on April 3, 1990. Moon had just recorded its declination maximum one day prior. Assuming a 6:45 a.m. first trade time, the Ascendant is 90-degrees square to the 1882 New York Mercantile Exchange natal Ascendant. Both Mercury and Moon were at their maximum declinations.

Applying the Periodogram function to the daily price chart of Natural Gas futures reveals a few dominant cycles: 514, 561, and 654 days. These align to:

- 8 ¾ Mercury axial spins (513 days) which is a near-exact match to the 514-day cycle.
- 9 ½ Mercury axial spins (557 days) which is a close match to the 561-day cycle.
- 7 ½ Mercury orbits around the Sun (660 days) which is reasonably close to the 654-day cycle.
- 11 ¼ Mercury axial spins (660 days) which is likewise reasonably close to the 654-day cycle.

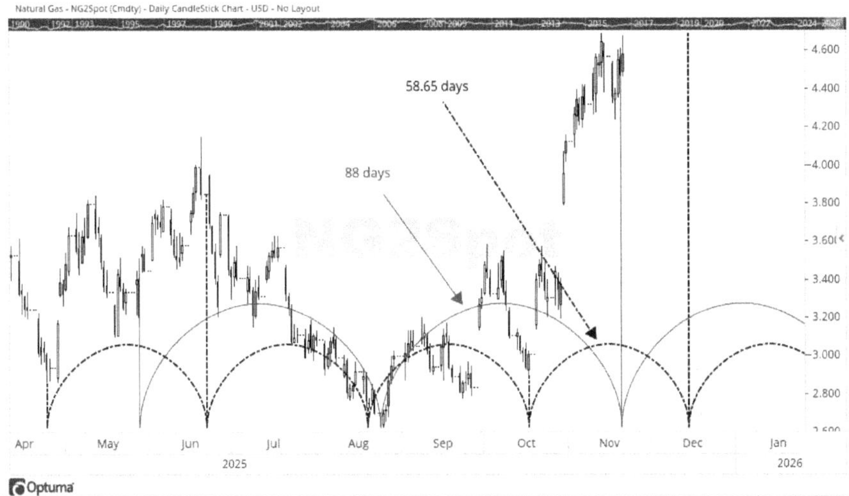


**Figure 9-27**
Natural Gas futures with Mercury cycles

The daily price chart in Figure 9-27 has been fitted with Mercury axial spin cycles and Mercury orbital cycles.

Traders and investors of natural-gas-related stocks can project forward by 88-day increments from around November 20, 2025 to identify points of interest in 2026. For the Mercury axial spin cycles, projecting forward in 58.65-day increments from December 15, 2025 will identify points of interest in 2026.

## New York Coffee Exchange

During the U.S. Civil War, the federal government in Washington was a major buyer of coffee beans. Coffee imports in those years came via Dutch and British suppliers. Following the war, demand for coffee dropped, as did prices. Several years of adverse weather around the globe then created speculative fervor causing prices to trade wildly up and down. To gain control over pricing, a group of coffee importing merchants established a coffee exchange in New York.

Coffee futures contracts started trading on the newly formed New York Coffee Exchange on March 7, 1882. On this date, Mercury had just turned stationary after having been retrograde. The Mid-Heaven at 14 Capricorn was 90-degrees square to the NYSE natal Ascendant point. Evidently some careful thought was applied to selecting this first trade date in 1882.

Applying the Periodogram function to the daily price chart of Coffee futures reveals several dominant cycles: 488, 544, 619, and 698 days. These align to:

- 5 ½ Mercury orbits around the Sun (484 days) which closely match the 488-day cycle.
- 9 ¼ axial spins of Mercury (542 days) which is a very close match to the 544-day cycle.
- 7 Mercury orbits around the Sun (616 days) which is a close match to the 619-day cycle.
- 8 Mercury orbits around the Sun (704 days) which is a close match to the 698-day cycle.

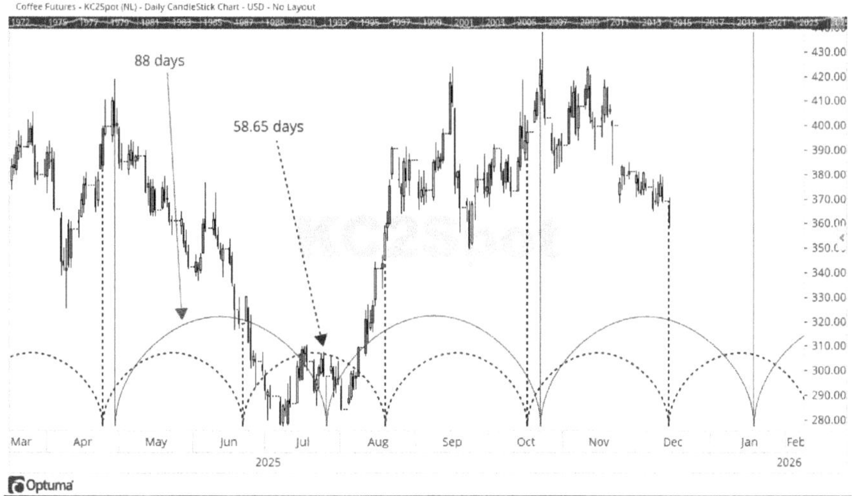


**Figure 9-28**
Coffee futures with Mercury cycles

The Coffee futures chart in Figure 9-28 has been fitted with Mercury orbital cycles and also Mercury axial cycles. Note how the swing high in October 2025 came in close alignment to an axial cycle and an orbital cycle.

Traders with an interest in Coffee futures can project forward in 88-day increments from around October 22, 2025 to identify points of interest in 2026. From mid-December 2025, projecting forward by 58.65-day increments will identify additional points of interest in 2026.

## New York Coffee and Sugar Exchange

Sugar as a bulk commodity started trading in New York as early as 1881. However, interest in trading Sugar in the U.S. was tepid; the majority of Sugar trades were being done in Hamburg and London.

After WW I hostilities ceased, a renewed effort was made to trade Sugar contracts in New York. Unable to raise enough money to build a dedicated Sugar exchange, interested parties convinced the New York Coffee Exchange to host a Sugar futures contract. On August 29, 1916, the New York Coffee Exchange changed its name to the New York Coffee and Sugar Exchange. This date seems to have been chosen because Moon and Venus were both at 0-degrees declination. In addition, Sun and Moon were both in the sign of Virgo.

Applying the Periodogram function to the daily price chart of Sugar futures reveals a dominant cycle of 680 days. This is in very close alignment to the time for Mars to orbit one time around the Sun (687 days).

The daily Sugar futures price chart in Figure 9-29 has been fitted with 687-day Mars cycles. In addition, the 3rd harmonic divisions (230 days) have been added.

Note how a price pivot point in July 2024, another one in February 2025, and yet another in October 2025 all aligned to these harmonic intervals. Late May of 2026 will deliver another of these harmonic intervals. After that, mid-January 2027 will bring the next interval. The larger 687-day cycle will not terminate until mid-August of 2027.

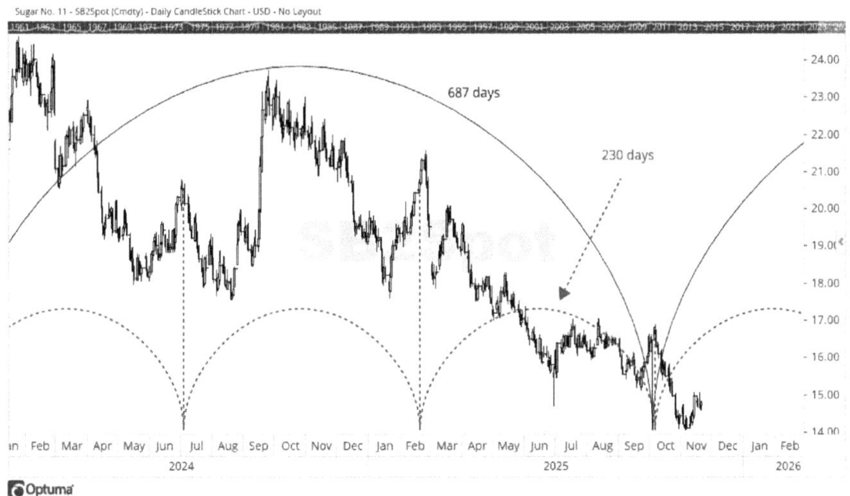


**Figure 9-29**
Sugar futures with Mars orbital cycles

# New York Cocoa Exchange

As early as the U.S. War of Independence, cocoa was being imported into the American colonies. However, it would not be until 1925 that a formal futures exchange would be established in New York to handle Cocoa futures. Cocoa futures contracts started trading in New York on October 1, 1925. On this date, Mercury was closing in on 0-degrees declination, Venus was at its declination minimum, Moon was at 0-degrees declination, and Mercury was at maximum latitude. and Mars were at 0-degrees declination. Assuming a 6:30 a.m. first trade time, the Ascendant point was 90-degrees square to the NYSE natal Ascendant point of 14 Cancer.

Applying the Periodogram function to the daily price chart of Cocoa futures reveals a single dominant cycle of 512 days. This aligns to:

- 8 ¾ Mercury axial spins (513 days) which is a near match.
- 2 ¼ Venus orbits around the Sun (506 days) is within a 1% margin of error.
- 0.75 Mars orbits around the Sun (515 days) is also a very close match.

The Cocoa futures chart in Figure 9-30 has been fitted with a Venus orbital cycle, Mercury axial spin cycles and also the 4$^{th}$ harmonic of a Mars orbital cycle.

Traders with an interest in Cocoa futures can project forward in 225-day increments from around July 17, 2025 to identify Venus cycle points of interest in 2026 (around March 1 and again around mid-October, 2026). From mid-October 2025, forward projections of 172-days place Mars 4$^{th}$ harmonic intervals at early April, and late-September 2026. Projecting forward by 58.65-day increments from around December 10, 2025 will identify additional Mercury axial spin cycles.

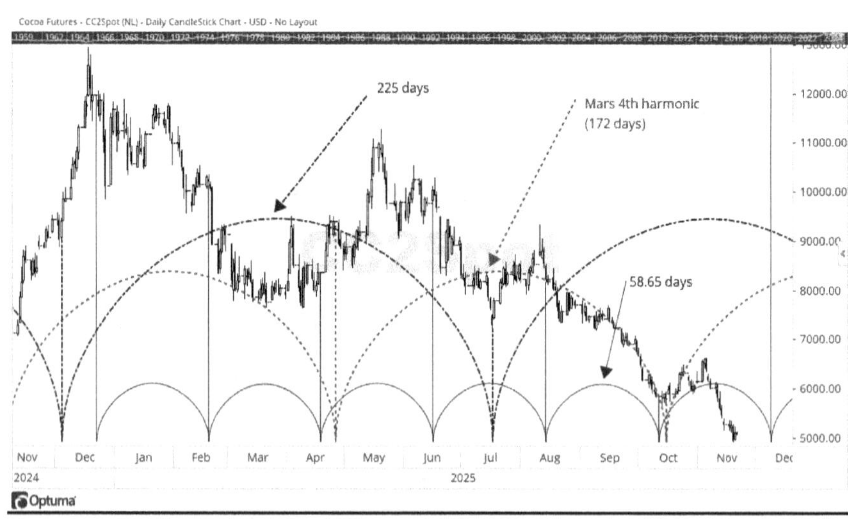


**Figure 9-30**
Cocoa futures with Mars, Venus, and Mercury cycles

# Indices and ETFs

## China

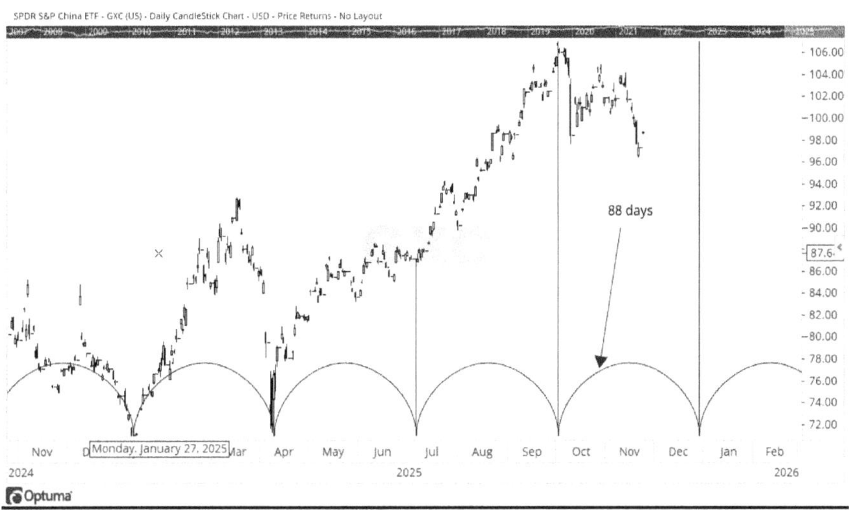


**Figure 9-31**
SPDR China ETF and Mercury orbital cycles

Applying the Periodogram function to the daily price chart of the SPDR China ETF reveals dominant cycles of 326 and 283 days. These time periods align to:

- 3 ¼ orbital periods of Mercury around the Sun (286 days).
- 3 ¾ orbital periods of Mercury around the Sun (330 days).

The daily chart in Figure 9-31 has been fitted with Mercury orbital cycles. Traders and investors with an interest in the Chinese market can project forward in 88-day increments from December 30, 2025 to identify the cycles in 2026.

# EuroStoxx

**Figure 9-32**
SPDR Eurostoxx 50 ETF and Mercury orbital cycles

Applying the Periodogram function to the daily price chart of the SPDR Eurostoxx 50 ETF (ticker symbol FEZ) reveals dominant cycles of 415, 438, and 623 days. These time periods align to:

- 4 ¾ orbital periods of Mercury around the Sun (418 days).
- 5 orbital periods of Mercury around the Sun (440 days).
- 7 orbital periods of Mercury around the Sun (616 days) which is within a 1% margin of error.

The daily chart in Figure 9-32 has been fitted with Mercury orbital cycles. Traders and investors with an interest in the Euro market can project forward in 88-day increments from January 14, 2026 to identify further cycles in 2026.

# Australia

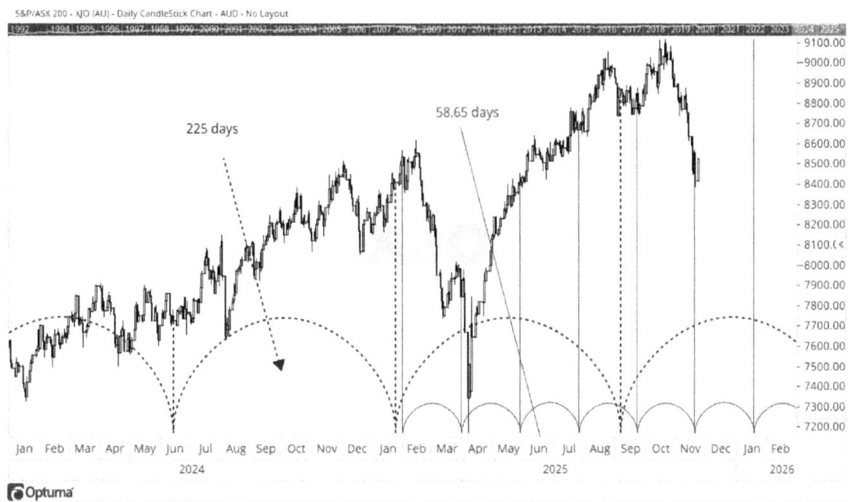


**Figure 9-33**
Australian ASX 200 with Venus and Mercury axial spin cycles

Applying the Periodogram function to the daily price chart of the Australian ASX 200 (ticker symbol XJO) reveals dominant cycles of 453, 528, and 588 days. These time periods align to:

- 2 orbital periods of Venus around the Sun (450 days).
- 9 axial spins of Mercury (528 days).
- 10 axial spins of Mercury (586 days).

The daily chart in Figure 9-33 has been fitted with Venus orbital cycles and Mercury axial spin cycles. Traders and investors with an interest in the Australian market can project forward in 225-day increments from around September 6, 2025 to identify further Venus cycles in 2026. Projections of 58.65 day increments from January 18, 2026 will identify additional Mercury axial spin cycles.

# Canadian Equities

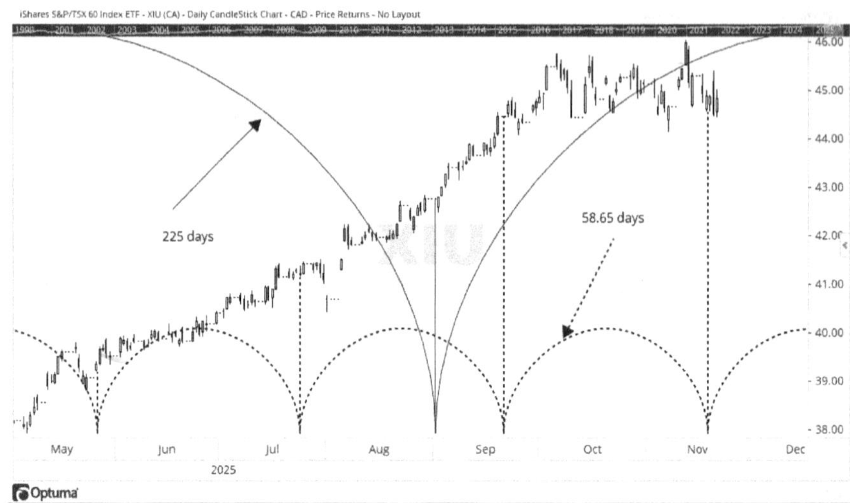


**Figure 9-34**

S&P TSX 60 with Venus and Mercury axial spin cycles

Applying the Periodogram function to the daily price chart of the Canadian iShares S&P TSX 60 (ticker symbol XIU) reveals dominant cycles of 455, 495, and 526 days. These time periods align to:

- 2 orbital periods of Venus around the Sun (450 days).
- 8 ½ axial spins of Mercury (498 days).
- 9 axial spins of Mercury (528 days).

The daily chart in Figure 9-34 has been fitted with Venus orbital cycles and Mercury axial spin cycles. Traders and investors with an interest in the largest 60 stocks that trade on the Toronto Exchange can project forward in 225-day increments from around September 1, 2025 to identify further Venus cycles in 2026. Projections of 58.65 day increments from January 15, 2026 will identify additional Mercury axial spin cycles.

# Canadian Gold Miners

Applying the Periodogram function to the daily price chart of the Canadian iShares Gold Miners (ticker symbol XGD) reveals dominant cycles of 427, 473, 507, and 619 days. These time periods align to:

- 7 ¼ axial spins of Mercury (425 days).
- 8 axial spins of Mercury (470 days).
- 5 ¾ Mercury orbits around the Sun (506 days).
- 7 Mercury orbits around the Sun (616 days).

The daily chart in Figure 9-35 has been fitted with Mercury orbital cycles and Mercury axial spin cycles. Traders and investors with an interest in gold mining stocks in Canada can project forward in 88-day increments from around December 18, 2025 to identify further Mercury cycles in 2026. Projections of 58.65 day increments from around December 13, 2025 will identify additional Mercury axial spin cycles.

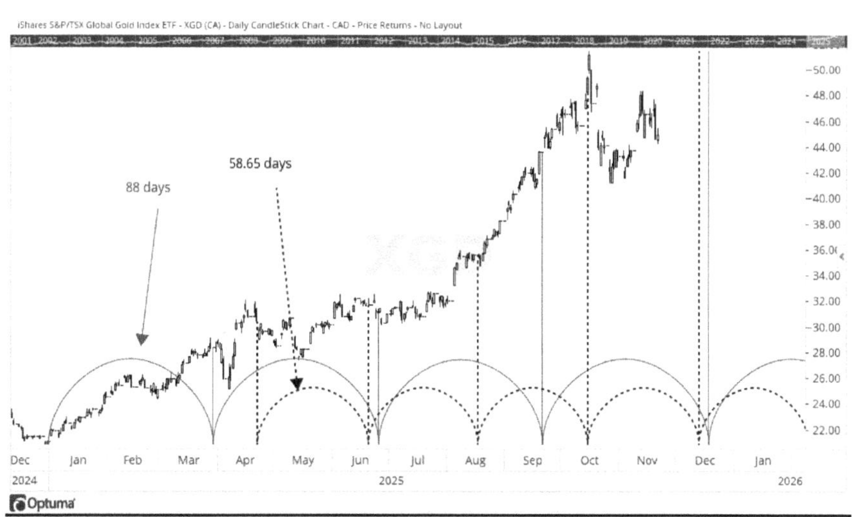


**Figure 9-35**
iShares Canadian Gold miners Mercury cycles

# Canadian Energy Index

Applying the Periodogram function to the daily price chart of the Canadian Energy Index (ticker symbol XEG) reveals dominant cycles of 501, 523, 587, and 618 days. These time periods align to:

- 5 ¾ orbits of Mercury around the Sun (506 days).
- 9 axial spins of Mercury (528 days).
- 10 axial spins of Mercury (586 days).
- 7 Mercury orbits around the Sun (616 days).

The daily chart in Figure 9-36 has been fitted with Mercury orbital cycles and Mercury axial spin cycles. Traders and investors with an interest in energy producing stocks in Canada can project forward in 88-day increments from around December 28, 2025 to identify further Mercury cycles in 2026. Projections of 58.65 day increments from around December 16, 2025 will identify additional Mercury axial spin cycles.

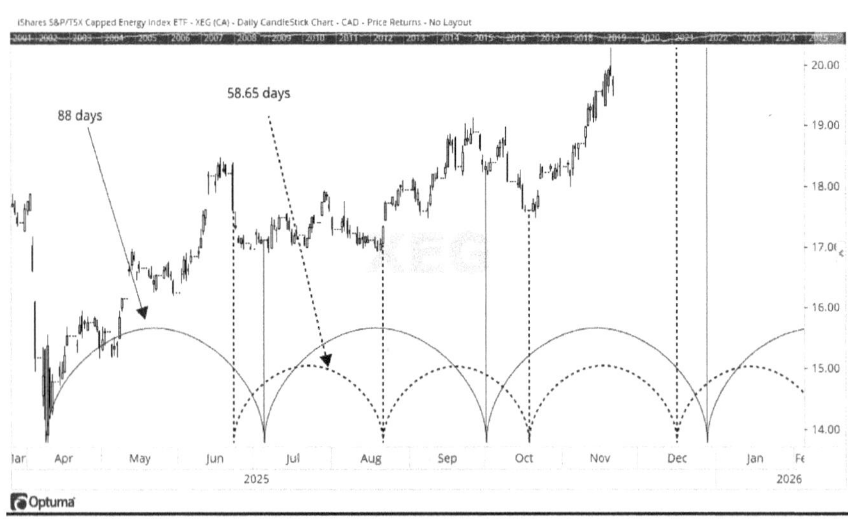


**Figure 9-36**

iShares Canadian energy stocks with Mercury cycles

# CHAPTER TEN

## *Longer Cycles*

### The 18.6-Year Cycle

In addition to cycles that align to the orbital periods and axial spin times of planets, there are longer cycles that influence human emotion. Key among these cycles is a geocentric one involving the Moon.

Ancient civilizations were acutely aware of an 18.6-year cycle involving the Moon. In the final month, near the terminus of this cycle, the position of the Moon in the night sky is at an extreme range of declination; the minimum declination event has the Moon low above the horizon while the declination maximum event has the Moon high in the sky. Many megalithic archeological sites around the world are structured to observe the end of this cycle.

This cycle led astrologers to identify two mathematical features in the geocentric zodiac called the *Nodes*. The Moon orbits the Earth in a plane of motion called the *lunar ecliptic.* The Earth's ecliptic plane, not being parallel to the lunar ecliptic plane, intersects the lunar plane at two points. The two points are termed the *North Node* and *South Node* and are opposite one another in the zodiac wheel. Common practice among practitioners of classical astrology is to focus only on the North Node.

Astronomers have a complex algorithm that allows them to calculate the positions of the Nodes. The Nodes move retrograde (backwards) through the twelve signs of the zodiac wheel and complete a full journey through the signs in 18.6 years.

## Louise McWhirter

The 18.6-year cycle in the context of economics was popularized in the late 1930s by Louise McWhirter, a little-known-about astrologer from New York city. Through examination of copious amounts of economic data provided by Leonard P. Ayers of the Cleveland Trust Company, McWhirter was able to conclude that when the North Node moves through certain zodiac signs, the economic business cycle reaches a low point. When the Node is passing certain other signs, the business cycle is at its strongest.

McWhirter was able to discern the following from the Cleveland Trust data:

- As the Node enters Aquarius, a low point of economic activity is manifesting
- As the Node leaves Aquarius and begins to transit through Capricorn and Sagittarius, the economy starts to return to normal
- As the Node passes through Scorpio and Libra, the economy is functioning at an above-normal tempo

- As the Node transits through Leo, a high point in economic activity is evident
- As the Node transits through Cancer and Gemini, the economy begins easing back towards a normal level of activity
- As the Node enters the sign of Taurus, the economy begins to slow
- As the Node enters Aquarius, the low point of economic activity is reached and a full 18.6-year cycle is completed.

McWhirter further observed some secondary factors that stand to influence the tenor of economic activity in a *good* way, regardless of which sign the Node is in at the time:

- Jupiter being 0-degrees conjunct to the Node
- Jupiter being in the sign of Gemini or Cancer
- Pluto being at a favorable aspect to the Node.

McWhirter also observed some secondary factors that can influence the tenor of economic activity in a *bad* way, regardless of which sign the Node is in at the time:

- Saturn being 0, 90, or 180-degrees to the Node
- Saturn in the signs of Gemini or Cancer
- Uranus in Gemini
- Uranus being 0, 90 or 180-degrees to the Node
- Pluto being at an unfavorable aspect to the Node.

## The Current 18.6 Year Cycle

The Node entered the sign of Pisces in February 2025–a reminder that the current 18.6-year cycle is getting long in the tooth and the economy is slowing. This reminder was underscored in April 2025 when political leadership in Washington imposed steep tariffs on imported goods. These tariffs caused consumer prices to rise. Data since the tariff application has shown that indeed the economy is slowing.

Despite this slowing theme, Jupiter was in the sign of Gemini until early June 2025 which, according to McWhirter's data, should have given a generally positive tone to the economy. However, along the way Saturn muddied the waters in the April-May 2025 period when it recorded a 0-degree hard aspect to the Node. When U.S. political leadership made mean-spirited moves to raise tariffs on goods from a number of countries, the Saturn influence was on full display.

In August 2026, the Node will be in Aquarius which will mark the final portion of the 18.6-year cycle and a low point in economic activity. A possible trigger for a crisis event could be defaults on private credit. Tighter banking regulations have resulted in large financial institutions promoting private credit as a new portfolio asset class. As 2025 neared an end, default rates on private credit loans were on the rise. Traders and investors should not be surprised to see another financial crisis in late 2026 and into 2027 that potentially rivals the one experienced in 2008, especially if concerns over private credit defaults spills over into the regional banking sector.

There is an old adage, attributed to 1940s British Prime Minister Wilson Chuchill, that says 'never let a good crisis go to waste'. Some legislative moves in July 2025 point to the possibility of major policy shifts in the U.S. that could take advantage of the coming end of the 18.6 year cycle. In July, President Trump signed into law the GENIUS Act – the *Guiding and Establishing National Innovation for U.S. Stablecoins Act.* The Act states that stablecoins must be backed 1:1 by high-quality, liquid reserve assets, such as U.S. dollars, U.S. Treasury bills with short maturities, or other cash-equivalent instruments. Regulators have been tasked to finish creating the policy guardrails around stablecoins by late 2026.

While the mainstream media has been silent on the topic of stablecoins, some concerns are starting to be expressed by independent financial bloggers. For example, suppose that stablecoins backed by U.S. Treasury debt prove to be solidly popular. The U.S. government could then expand its debt in a prolific way, setting the stage for a future economic dilemma.

## The 18.6 Year Cycle and Heliocentric Events

In past issues of this Almanac, McWhirter's work was approached purely from a geocentric perspective. Significant variability was noted regarding the timing of equity market tops and bottoms in the context of the Node in Pisces and Aquarius. A heliocentric look at past events of Node entering Aquarius provides more insight.

### 1952

The Node entered Aquarius on March 6, 1952. Leading up to this event, the U.S. economy was resilient and still enjoying the post-World War 2 economic boom. With the Node at 13 Aquarius on January 4, 1953, the Dow Jones Average began a modest drawdown of 13 percent. The trigger for the start of this decline seems to have been: Venus 0-degrees conjunct to Jupiter, Venus 60-degrees to Earth, Venus 180-degrees opposite Mercury, and Mercury 120-degrees to Earth.

In mid-September, 1953 with the Node almost through its transit of Aquarius, the market decided to begin a three-year bullish run. The trigger for this was a collision of heliocentric events: Saturn 120-degrees to Venus, Venus 0-degrees to Jupiter, Venus/Jupiter 90-degrees to Mercury, Venus/Jupiter 90-degrees to Earth, and Earth 180-degrees to Mercury. In addition, Moon was at its declination minimum, Mercury was at 0-degrees declination, and Venus was at its declination maximum.

## 1970

The Node next entered Aquarius on October 16, 1970. The Dow Jones Average had already recorded a significant drawdown starting in early December of 1968 with Node at 6 Aries. Why the early market response? A look at the heliocentric zodiac wheel reveals that the drawdown was sparked by Earth being 90-degrees square to Jupiter, Mercury 180-degrees opposite to Earth, Venus 180-degrees opposite to Jupiter, Saturn 120-degrees to Mercury, and Saturn 150-degrees to Jupiter. In addition, Venus was at 0-degrees declination and Moon was at its maximum declination.

## 1989

The Node next entered Aquarius on May 29, 1989. However, the Dow Jones Average had already recorded a sell-off starting in late August 1987 with the Node at 2 degrees Aries. The heliocentric zodiac wheel reveals that the early drawdown was sparked by Saturn being 120-degrees to Jupiter, Earth 180-degrees opposite to Venus, and Saturn 90-degrees square to Mercury. Moon and Mercury were both at 0-degrees declination as well. This sharp sell-off came to an end on October 21, 1987 with Earth and Jupiter being 0-degrees conjunct, the pair being 120-degrees trine to Saturn, and Venus being 120-degrees trine to Mercury.

## 2008

The Node next entered Aquarius on January 7, 2008. However, the Dow Jones Average had already recorded a peak on October 11, 2007 with Node at 4 Pisces. Why the early market response? At the October market peak, Jupiter was 120-degrees trine to Saturn, Mercury was 90-degrees square to Venus, Mercury was 180-degrees opposite Saturn, and Jupiter was 60-degrees to Mercury. When the selloff carnage ended in early March 2009, Earth was 0-degrees conjunct to Saturn, Venus was nearing in on a 0-degree aspect to Earth, Mercury was approaching a 0-degree aspect to Jupiter, Jupiter was 120-degrees to Venus. Mercury was at its declination minimum and Moon was at its maximum declination.

## 2026

Node will next enter Aquarius on August 18, 2026. Leading up to this event, Jupiter will leave its favorable position in Cancer in early July 2026. Uranus will be in the sign of Gemini and 90-degrees square to the Node. Traders and investors should be alert for signs of economic and market weakness. The chances of a significant market meltdown are to be taken seriously.

As the geocentric Node enters Aquarius, heliocentric Venus will be 180-degrees opposite to Mercury and Jupiter will be 120-degrees trine to Saturn. These events could well be sufficient to sway human emotion and cause the equity market to react. Several weeks later, towards the end of September, Earth and Saturn will be within 8-degrees of being conjunct to one another, Earth will be conjunct Jupiter, and Saturn will be 120-degrees trine to Jupiter. Mercury will be 120-degrees trine to Jupiter and also trine to Saturn. On October 4, 2026 Earth and Saturn will be exactly conjunct. The pair will be 120-degrees trine to Jupiter and the pair will be 90-degrees square to Mercury.

## The War Cycle

In addition to the 18.6-year nodal cycle, there is another long cycle with more profound implications – the Uranus war cycle.

Geocentric Uranus takes about 85 years to move through the signs of the zodiac. The 1776 natal horoscope for the United States of America has Uranus at 8 degrees of the sign of Gemini. Subsequent cycles of Uranus passing this Gemini point have resulted in conflict (Civil War and World War 2).

In August 2025, Uranus entered the sign of Gemini. This timeframe marked the start of a deeper U.S. naval involvement in the Caribbean region off the coast of Venezuela. Over one dozen so-called drug smuggling boats were subsequently shot at and destroyed. In September 2025, Uranus turned retrograde and retreated into the sign of Taurus. Uranus will again enter Gemini in April 2026 and will spend the next seven years moving through the sign. By mid-2027 Uranus will be exactly conjunct to the 1776 Uranus natal position at 8 degrees of Gemini.

One need not look too hard to see how fragile the global geopolitical situation is. A 2027 conflict of some sort could well be in the making now. The Russia-Ukraine conflict shows possible signs of abating towards the end of 2025, but with a distinct advantage to Vladimir Putin. The Israel-Gaza-Hamas situation is sitting on a tenuous ceasefire which could yet fail. Iran remains a rogue state as does North Korea. And China has wider geopolitical ambitions.

## The Gann Master Cycle

W.D. Gann closely followed the cycles of Jupiter and Saturn. To an observer situated on the fixed (heliocentric) vantage point of the Sun, Jupiter can be seen orbiting the Sun in about 12 years and Saturn in just over 29 years. Gann interpreted these orbital cycles one step further and noted that every 19.86 years, heliocentric Jupiter and Saturn were at a 0-degree conjunction. This 19.86-year time span is what he called the *Master Cycle.*

The curious feature of the Master Cycle is that the occurrence of the Jupiter/Saturn conjunction does not always align precisely with a change of market trend. Interfering in the background are geopolitical events and Central Bank policy decisions. Also at work are heliocentric planetary aspects. Consider the following examples:

- The market weakness in late 1901 aligned to a conjunction of Saturn and Jupiter. But following this conjunction event, the Dow Jones remained bearish and did not reach a definitive turning point low until mid-November 1903 when the two planets were 45-degrees apart. A look at the heliocentric zodiac offers insight. The 1903 market low came as Saturn was 120-degrees trine to Venus, Venus was 120-degrees trine Mercury, Mercury was 120-degrees trine Saturn, and Saturn was 90-degrees to Earth. In addition, Venus was at its declination maximum, Mercury was at 0-degrees declination, and Moon was at its declination maximum.

- In 1920, the U.S. economy encountered a recession. In August 1921, Jupiter and Saturn reached exact conjunction. After this conjunction, the Dow Jones started to rally higher almost as if on cue aided by Earth being 180-degrees to Mercury, and Jupiter/Saturn being 120-degrees to Mercury. Moon was at its declination maximum.

  As an aside, the September 1929 market peak was not related to the Gann Master Cycle. However, it did come with Earth 90-degrees to Jupiter, Earth 90-degrees to Venus, Earth 90-degrees to Mercury, Mercury 180-degrees to Jupiter, and Mercury 180-degrees to Venus. Venus was closing in on its declination maximum; Mercury was at its declination minimum, and Moon was at 0-degrees declination. The dramatic sell-off ended on November 13, 1929 when sellers were exhausted. The recovery rally that followed ran out of momentum by April 15, 1930 when aspects of Earth 120-degrees to Jupiter, Venus 0-degrees to Jupiter, and Earth 90-degrees to Mercury all combined to sway human emotion and trigger more weakness. Moon was at its declination minimum; Mercury was at its declination maximum, and Venus was closing in on its declination maximum. It would not be until early July 1932 when the selling finally came to an end. Human emotion at this point was impacted by Earth being 0-degrees to both Venus and Saturn and Saturn being 90-degrees to Mercury. Venus was at its declination minimum, Mercury was at 0-degees declination, and Moon was at 0-degrees declination.

- By May 1940, Jupiter and Saturn were within 10-degrees of one another and were on their way to a conjunction in July 1940. The Dow Jones recorded a 22% drawdown starting in early May of 1940. This early start to market weakness was augmented by Earth 120-degrees to Mercury and Venus 180-degrees to Jupiter. Moon was at its declination maximum, and both Mercury and Venus were passing 0-degrees declination. Despite several efforts at recovering, the market trend remained bearish until late April 1942 when human emotion changed due to Mercury and Jupiter being 0-degrees apart and the pair being 180-degrees to Venus. Moon was at 0-degrees declination, Mercury was at its declination maximum, and Venus was at its declination minimum.

- In late April 1961, Jupiter and Saturn again were at a 0-degree conjunction. Despite the conjunction, the Dow Jones continued to advance. In late May, Mercury 120-degrees to Venus and Earth 60-degrees to Jupiter and Saturn caused a shift in emotion, but the Dow recovered and kept advancing. Finally, the Dow Jones reached a turning point in mid-November 1961 at a Venus and Mercury conjunction. Moon was at 0-degrees declination and both Venus and Mercury were closing in on their declination minima.

- In April 1981, Jupiter and Saturn recorded a conjunction event which aligned to a peak in the Dow Jones Average. The ensuing bearish trend lasted until August 1982 when the Dow Jones recorded a turning point low that evolved into a massive bull market run that endured (despite the 1987 brief, but severe, sell-off) until the next Jupiter-Saturn conjunction event in June 2000. The August 1982 turning point had a collision of heliocentric events at play: Earth at 120-degrees to both Saturn and Mercury, Earth 90-degrees to Jupiter, Earth 120-degrees to Venus, and Venus 120-degrees to both Saturn and Mercury. In addition, Venus was at its declination maximum, Mercury was at 0-degrees declination as was the Moon.

- In June of 2000, Jupiter and Saturn recorded a conjunction event. However, the Dow Jones Average had already recorded a peak in mid-January 2000 when the two planets were still 8-degrees apart. Why the early response by the market? At the time of the market peak, Earth was 180-degrees opposite Mercury, Earth was 90-degrees square Venus, and Mercury made 90-degree square aspects to Saturn and Jupiter. All of these events collaborated to maximize gravitational torque on the Sun's outer layers. In addition, Moon was at 0-degrees declination, Mercury was at 0-degrees declination, and Venus had just passed through 0-degrees declination.

- Following the January 2000 onset of a bearish trend, it would not be until October 10, 2002 when the bearish mindset abated and the Dow Jones reached a turning point low. Contributing to the 2002 turning point was Venus drawing to within 10-degrees of Earth, Mercury recording a conjunction to Saturn, and Venus being 120-degrees to Jupiter. Moon was at minimum declination, Mercury was at its maximum declination, and Venus was at 0-degrees declination.

- In November 2020, heliocentric Saturn and Jupiter again made their 0-degree conjunction right at the time of the U.S. Presidential election. But the market had already recorded a significant low point several months beforehand in late March when the two planets were 12-degrees apart. This particular turning point was the COVID panic selloff. The trigger for the start of the COVID panic selloff in February was Mercury approaching a 0-degree conjunction with Earth, Earth 120-degrees to Jupiter, and Venus 180-degrees to Jupiter. Moon was at 0-degrees declination, Mercury at declination maximum, and Venus at declination maximum.

- The next Saturn-Jupiter conjunction event will occur in December of 2040. If you are examining this manuscript in 2040, you might have seen the overall trend change several months before this conjunction date. In late June 1940,

Mercury will be conjunct Earth and the pair will be 90-degrees square to Saturn and Jupiter (7-degrees apart at the time).

## Professor Weston

In 1921, a mysterious person from Washington, D.C. using the name Professor Weston wrote a paper in which he analyzed decades of past price data for the Dow Jones Average. Who exactly Weston was, will likely never be known; another one of those figures who emerged to write his ideas down before vanishing into the ether.

Perhaps Weston knew W.D. Gann personally, perhaps he just knew of him. In any case, Weston followed the 20-year Gann Master Cycle of Jupiter and Saturn. Weston also postulated that in the various years of a 10-year segment of the overall Master Cycle, there would be a series of market maxima. Weston's work brought into the current timeframe suggests there will be market maxima as follows: November 2025, June 2026, January and September 2027, June 2028, April 2029, February and August 2030. Weston determined these events using cycles of Venus. He argued that the 16$^{th}$ harmonic of a 10-year period (120 months) was actually the heliocentric time it takes for Venus to orbit the Sun (120 x 30 / 16 = 225 days). Weston's idea is supported by the fact that Periodogram analysis shows the S&P 500 to have a 446-day dominant cycle. This aligns to two heliocentric Venus orbits around the Sun (450 days).

## The Great Trigon Cycle

Triple recurrences of the Gann Master Cycle can have a pattern-like impact on geopolitics and on the financial markets. This pattern was first recognized in the early 1600s by Johhanes Kepler who noted that every 60 years Saturn and Jupiter would be 0-degrees conjunct at approximately the same zodiac degree sign. For example, *heliocentric*

Jupiter and Saturn were conjunct in April 1961 in the latter part of the sign of Capricorn. The 1981 conjunction occurred in the sign of Libra. The June 2000 conjunction occurred in the sign of Taurus. The November 2020 conjunction occurred at 0-degrees Aquarius, a mere 7-degrees from where the 1961 conjunction had occurred. These observations imply that every 60-years history can rhyme again. Consider the following examples of such rhythms:

- The U.S. equity market recorded its post-1929 crash low in 1932. Forward 60-years and 1982 marked the start of what would be a major bull market.
- The year 1937 marked an interim peak on the U.S. stock market. Forward 60-years and an interim peak followed by the 1997 Asian currency crisis comes into focus.
- A low was recorded on the market in 1942. Forward 60-years to 2002 and a similar event occurred.
- A low was again recorded in 1949. Forward 60-years and the March 2009 lows make an appearance.
- Late 1961 marked a turning point on the market. Forward 60-years and late 2021 likewise presented a turning point.
- The U.S. stock market recorded a peak in early 1966. Forward 60-years and early 2026 comes into view. The market reached a swing low in October 1966. Forward 60-years and October 2026 comes into focus.

It is further interesting to note that a 60-year rhythm can sometimes be seen outside of the financial markets. Consider the following:

Construction on the Pentagon building in Washington commenced on September 11, 1941. Forward 60-years and the September 11, 2001 terrorist attacks need no further explanation.

Early 1965 saw the first US ground troops land in Vietnam. This marked the start of what would be a decade-long simmering conflict. Forward 60-years and ask whether the geopolitical events (Ukraine, Iran, Gaza, Hamas, Lebanon, Hezbollah) that have unfolded during 2025 have set the stage for a multi-year simmering conflict?

# CHAPTER ELEVEN

## *George Bayer's Rules*

Very little is known about George Bayer, except that he was a German immigrant who arrived in New York around 1899. He came to America with considerable knowledge of the planets and our solar system. He wasted little time in opening a brokerage account in New York city and set to work trading agricultural futures contracts that traded in Chicago using his planetary knowledge to guide his buying and selling decisions. In the 1930s, after many years of making a comfortable living as a trader, he retired. Thankfully, he left a legacy in the form of his various Rules. What follows is a look at some of these rules. Even though some involve geocentric planetary phenomena and deviate from the heliocentric tenor of this Almanac, his Rules warrant serious examination by traders and investors.

## Rule #1 Geocentric Mercury Speed

Bayer's Rule # 1 says that when the geocentric speed of Mercury slows and turns negative, traders should watch for a price trend change. Figure 11-1 shows a daily chart of Wheat futures from mid-2024 to late-2025. The lower pane on the chart shows the geocentric speed of Mercury. Those periods of time when speed was below the zero line are denoted by rectangular boxes on the price chart. This example suggests that Bayer was indeed onto something when he penned this Rule. However, one must look a bit deeper. Why would the speed of Mercury as seen from our vantage point on Earth (geocentric) turn negative? The answer is – at times of Mercury retrograde. In fact, all of the rectangular boxes on the chart exactly denote Mercury retrograde events. As was discussed in an earlier chapter, the heliocentric equivalent to retrograde is when Mercury passes 0-degrees conjunct to Earth.

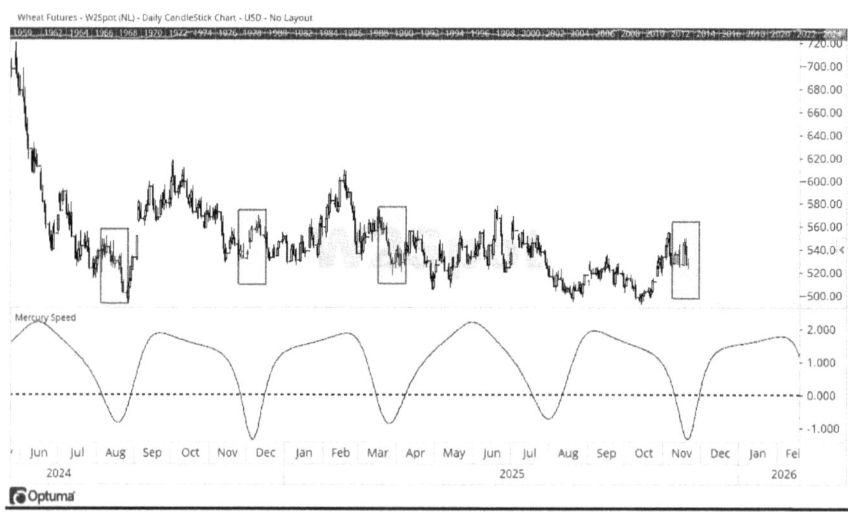


**Figure 11-1**
Bayer's Rule # 1 and Wheat futures

Bayer did not have access to the modern mathematical and astronomical studies discussed in this Almanac, but we now know that heliocentric Mercury at a 0-degree aspect to Earth imparts a maximum torque force on the Sun's surface layers which causes solar wind emissions which in turn can affect human emotion.

## Rule #7 Venus - Argument of Perihelion

Data from NASA indicates that the point where Venus comes closest to the Sun (perihelion) is at a longitude of 55-degrees as measured from the 0-degrees Aries point (the Spring equinox). This angular determination is also referred to as the *argument of perihelion.*

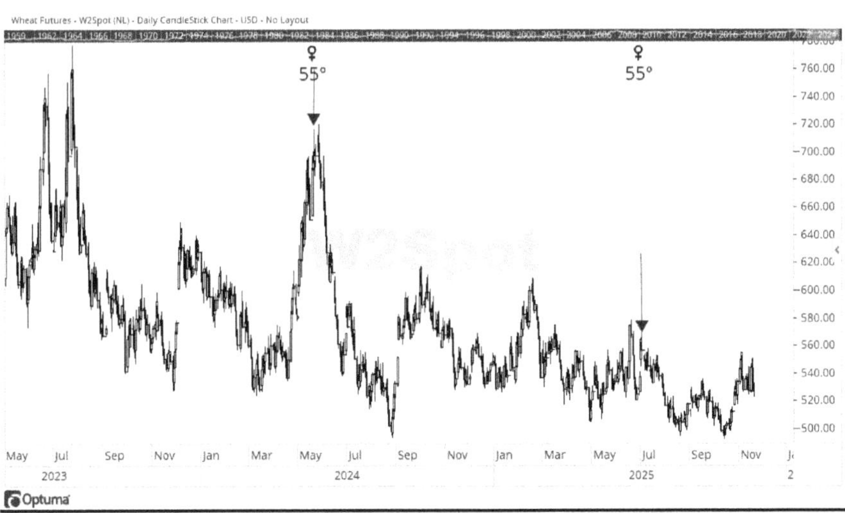


**Figure 11-2**
Bayer's Rule # 7 and Wheat futures

Bayer's Rule # 7 says to pay attention to the time when geocentric Venus passes 55-degrees of longitude. Figure 11-2 shows a daily chart of Wheat futures annotated with Venus 55-degree events. Again, Bayer seems to have been onto something. Bayer did not have access to the modern astronomical studies discussed in this Almanac, but we now know that inner planets at their closest approach to the Sun are capable of imparting torque forces to the Sun's surface layers which cause solar wind emissions.

## Rule #8 Venus - Argument of Perihelion (heliocentric)

Data from NASA indicates that the heliocentric point where Venus comes closest to the Sun (perihelion) is at a longitude of 126-degrees. Figure 11-3 shows a daily chart of Wheat futures annotated with heliocentric Venus 126-degree events. Bayer's Rule # 8 says to pay attention to the time when heliocentric Venus passes 126-degrees of longitude

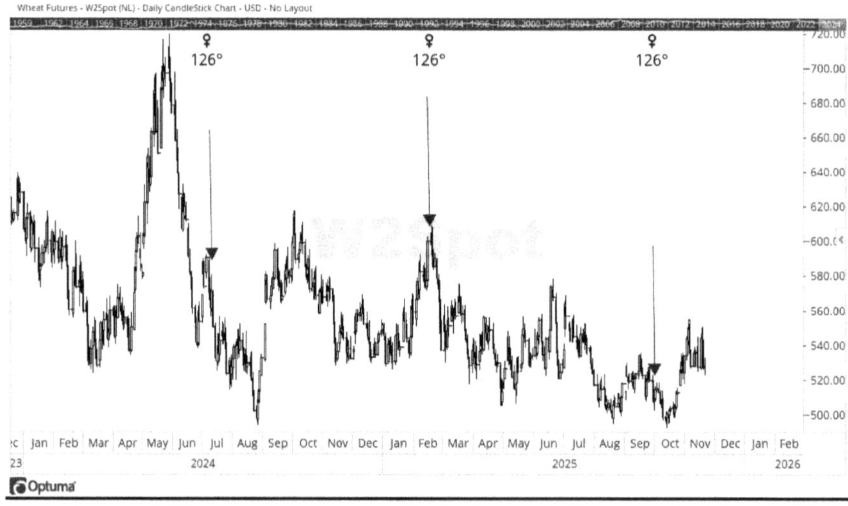


**Figure 11-3**
Bayer's Rule # 8 and Wheat futures

## Rule #17 Mercury Passing Two Key Zodiac Points

Rule #17 is one of Bayer's more archaic ideas. He states to identify the dates when geocentric Mercury is at 15 Aquarius (315 degrees) and 15 Leo (135 degrees). He states to make a note of the degree positions of the other planets at these dates. He then advises to identify the dates when Mercury will transit past these degree positions. He suggests these transits could result in a trend change. As archaic as this Rule is, it actually appears to work. Figure 11-4 presents a daily chart of Cotton futures from the 2024 period. Mercury was at 315 degrees in February 2024. Mercury was at 135 degrees in July 2024. The annotations on the chart show what other planets had degree positions greater than 315 or 135 degrees. Annotations then show when Mercury transited past these degree positions. The trend changes anticipated by this Rule could turn out to be short-term and small in scope. A trend-following chart indicator is essential if using this Rule.

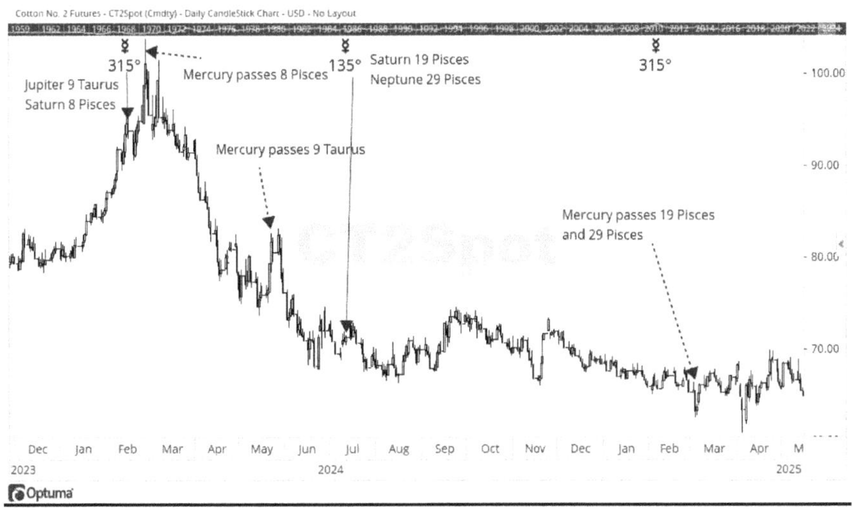


**Figure 11-4**
Bayer's Rule # 17 and Cotton futures

## Rule #19 Geocentric Venus Conjunct the Sun

Rule #19 says to pay attention to times when geocentric Venus passes conjunct to the Sun. In a heliocentric zodiac wheel, this transit is equivalent to Venus being 180-degrees opposite to Earth. The work of Scafetta and others has shown that Venus being opposite the Earth can induce a torque effect on the surface layers of the Sun which can result in an increased emission of solar wind particles. Figure 11-5 illustrates a chart of Wheat futures with events of heliocentric Venus opposite the Sun. The time frame covered by this chart is from late 2022 to mid-2024.

**Figure 11-5**
Bayer's Rule # 19 and Wheat futures

## Rule #22 Mercury Retrograde Conjunct to Sun

Rule #22 says to pay attention to events of Mercury retrograde passing conjunct to the Sun. From a heliocentric perspective, this is equivalent to events of Mercury conjunct to Earth. The work of Scafetta and others has shown that Mercury being conjunct the Earth can induce a torque effect on the surface layers of the Sun which can result in an increased emission of solar wind particles. The daily chart of Wheat futures in Figure 11-6 has been fitted with heliocentric events of Mercury conjunct Earth. The event of early August does not appear to align to a swing pivot reversal point. However, a closer look reveals that the conjunction came at the geocentric mean of the price decline that was occurring at the time.

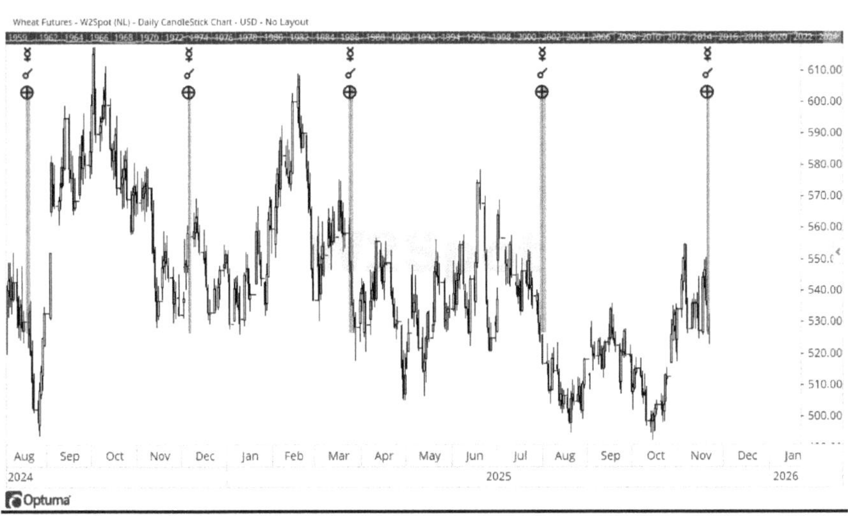


**Figure 11-6**
Bayer's Rule # 22 and Wheat futures

## Rule #27 Mercury Speed Extremes

Rule #27 seems to be an extension of Rule #1. In Rule #27, Bayer advises to pay attention to the times when Mercury is at its maximum orbital speed around the Sun. The Wheat futures chart in Figure 11-7 has been fitted with a plot of Mercury's speed in the lower pane. The one speed extrema that does not align to a price pivot point occurred in June 2024. However, a closer look at this event reveals it occurred at the geocentric mean of a price retracement event.

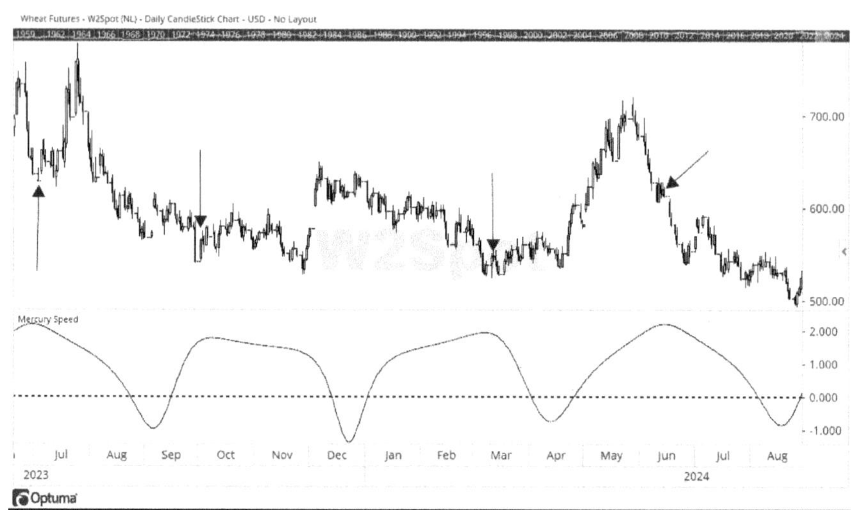


**Figure 11-7**
Bayer's Rule # 27 and Wheat futures

## Rule #32 Sun + 132 degrees

Rule #32 is another of Bayer's archaic creations. This Rule advises to identify a significant price top (or bottom) on a price chart. Note the geocentric longitude of the Sun at this top or bottom. Add 132 degrees to the longitude of the Sun. Next, look ahead in time to determine when Mercury will pass this calculated degree point.

Figure 11-8 illustrates this rule on a daily price chart of Cotton futures. From the top in late February 2024, the calculation points to a date in June 2024. The bearish selloff did subside at that date and Cotton prices entered period of sideways consolidation.

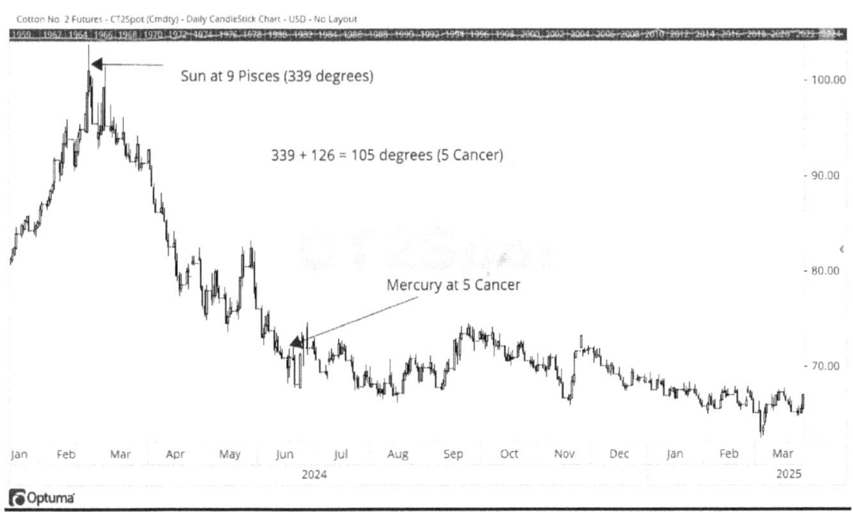


**Figure 11-8**
Bayer's Rule # 32 and Cotton futures

## Rule #36 Sun conjunct Mercury + 60 degrees

Rule #36 is yet another of Bayer's archaic creations. This Rule advises to identify times in a geocentric zodiac wheel when Sun and Mercury are conjunct. Add 60 degrees to this point. Next, look ahead in time to determine when Mercury will pass this calculated degree point. Figure 11-9 illustrates this rule on a daily price chart of Wheat futures. From the conjunction in early February 2025 at 21 Aquarius (321 degrees), an addition of 60 degrees takes one to 16 Aries in late April. The chart has been annotated to show Mercury passing the 16 of Aries point. As Bayer suggests will be the case, a trend change did occur.

**Figure 11-9**
Bayer's Rule # 36 and Wheat futures

## Rule #37 Sun conjunct Venus +60 degrees

Rule #37 is an extension of Rule #36. This Rule advises to determine a Sun conjunct Venus event. To the degree point of the event, add 60 degrees. Next look ahead in time to determine when Venus will pass this point.

Figure 11-10 illustrates this rule on a daily price chart of Wheat futures. From the conjunction in early June 2024 at 16 Gemini (86 degrees), an addition of 60 degrees takes one to 26 Leo in late April. The chart has been annotated to show Venus passing the 26 of Leo point. As Bayer suggests would be the case, a trend change did occur, although it was brief in length.

**Figure 11-10**
Bayer's Rule # 37 and Wheat futures

Figure 11-11 is a more recent example of Rule #37, again in the context of Wheat futures. From the conjunction event in March 2024, an increment of 60-degrees takes one to Venus at 1 degree of Gemini in early July which turned out to be a pivot point after which Wheat prices fell sharply.

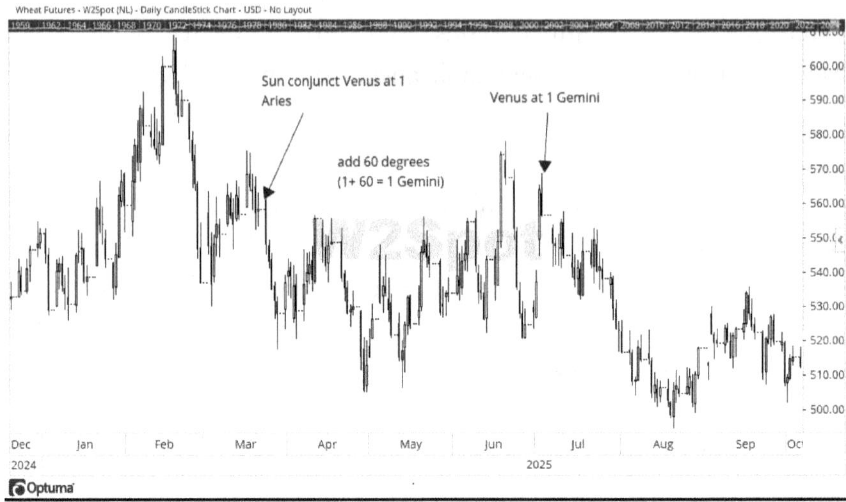


**Figure 11-11**
Bayer's Rule # 37 and Wheat futures

## Rule #48 Jupiter plus Right Ascension Time

Rule #48 delves into Right Ascension time. In this Rule, Bayer advises to identify a major price peak on a chart. He advises to note the heliocentric degree position of Jupiter at this price peak. He then advises to add 1 hour and 21 minutes of Right Ascension time to this degree position. The resulting date should align to a price trend change. In the heliocentric zodiac there are 24 hours of Right Ascension time. One hour of Right Ascension time therefore equals 15 degrees of the wheel. Adding 1 hour and 21 minutes of time is the same as adding 19.5 degrees to the position of Jupiter. The degree position of Jupiter at the March 2022 significant price high was 15 Pisces (345 degrees). Adding 19.5 degrees takes one to 4.5 degrees Aries.

The daily price chart of Wheat futures in Figure 11-12 has been annotated with an arrow to show when Jupiter was due at 4.5 degrees of Aries. The anticipated trend change was actually a failed countertrend rally attempt.

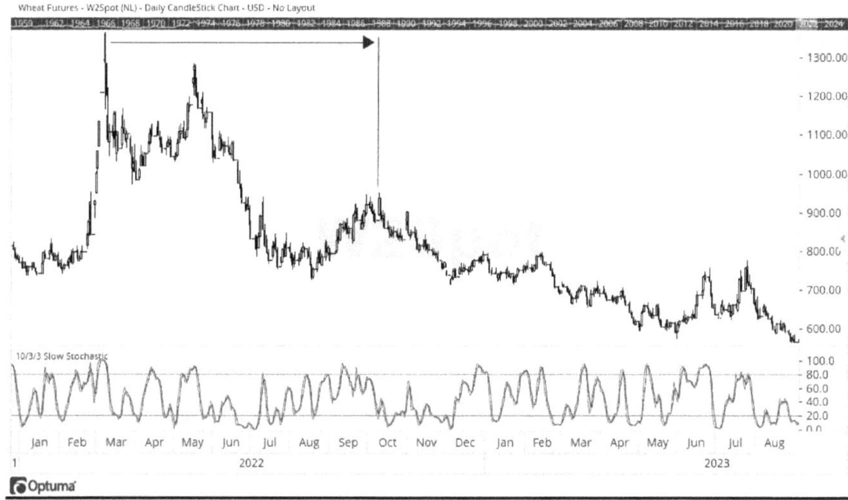


**Figure 11-12**
Bayer's Rule # 48 and Wheat futures

## Rule #9-A Mars Full Hour Right Ascension Times

Later in his trading career, Bayer seems to have penned eleven additional Rules (1-A through 11-A). Rule #9-A advises to focus on whole-hour intervals of Mars Right Ascension time.

Figure 11-13 shows a daily price chart of BitCoin futures fitted with vertical dashed lines depicting whole-hour increments in Right Ascension time. For example, if heliocentric Mars is at 0 degrees Libra (which it was on June 9, 2024), this equates to 180 zodiac degrees or 180/15 = 12 hours of Right Ascension time. The arrows denote subsequent whole-hour increments of Mars. Note how these arrows closely align to pivot swing points. The use of a trend indicator such as the Slow Stochastic will help keep one focused and in tune with the trend. The one exception is the arrow in mid-October, 2025. It actually landed at the geocentric mean of the price move lower in October. Once again, here is the mystery of the geocentric mean aligning to a planetary event.

**Figure 11-13**
Bayer's Rule # 9-A and BitCoin futures

## Rule #10-A Mars Right Ascension Plus 1.625 Hours

Bayer's Rule #10-A advises to identify a significant price high or low and from that point add 1 hour 37.5 minutes (equal to 1.625 hours) of Right Ascension time to the position of Mars.

Figure 11-14 is a daily chart of Wheat that has been fitted with this Rule starting from a price swing in May 2024. The projected intervals all align to trend swing points of various magnitudes.

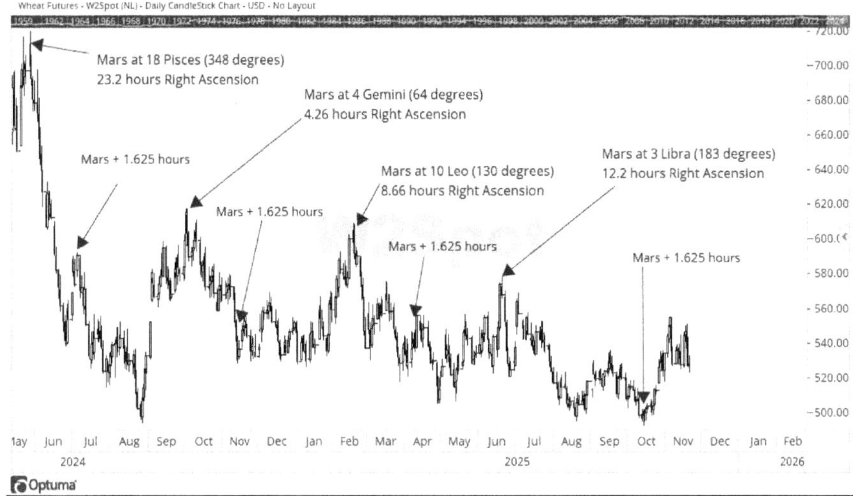


**Figure 11-14**
Bayer's Rule # 10-A and Wheat futures

Figure 11-15 is a daily chart of BitCoin futures that has been fitted with this Rule starting from a pivot point in July 2025. Forward projections of 1.625 R.A. hours of heliocentric Mars from subsequent peaks and valleys can be seen to align to swing pivot points.

**Figure 11-15**
Bayer's Rule # 10-A and BitCoin futures

## Rule #11-A Venus Right Ascension Plus 6.5 Hours

Bayer's Rule #11-A advises to identify a significant price high or low and from that point add 4 times 1 hour 37 minutes (equal to 6.5 hours) of Right Ascension time to the position of Venus.

Figure 11-16 is a daily chart of Wheat that has been fitted with this Rule starting from a series of price swing highs. The projected intervals all align to trend swing points of various magnitudes. November 20 and December 9, 2025 should both align to a pivot of some magnitude.

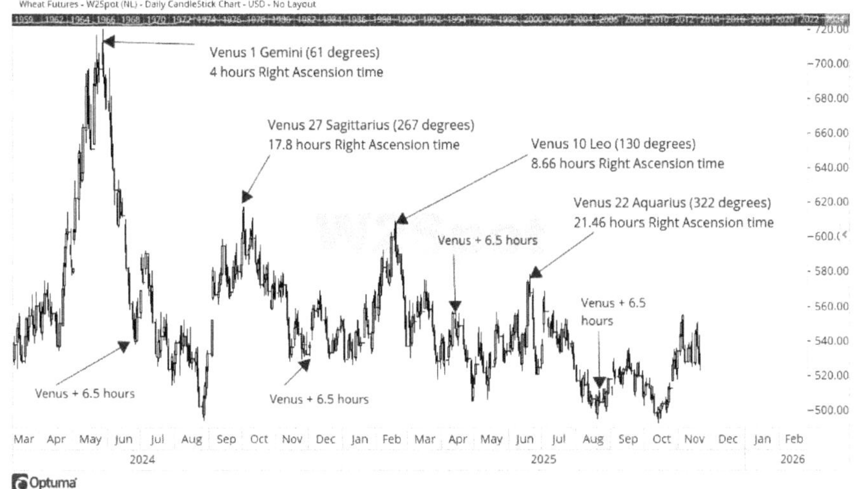


**Figure 11-16**
Bayer's Rule # 11-A and Wheat futures

**Figure 11-17**
Bayer's Rule # 11-A and BitCoin futures

Figure 11-17 is a daily chart of BitCoin futures that has been fitted with this Rule starting from a pivot point in July 2025. A forward projection of 6.5 R.A. hours of heliocentric Venus aligns to a pivot point in September 2025. Another 6.5 hour projection takes one to mid-November. A swing pivot point registered three days prior to this interval.

The key take-away with Rules #10-A and #11-A is traders and investors should consider applying both Rules to price charts to provide a clear picture of what lays ahead.

Bayer's Rules all take a certain amount of effort to apply. But the effort is worth it as these various examples have shown. If there is a point of frustration with Bayer's work, it is a lack of explanation as to how he arrived at some of his techniques. Perhaps one day soon someone will figure it out.

# CHAPTER TWELVE

## *2026 in Summary*

### January 2026

January starts off with Moon at its declination maximum and Mercury making a 120-degree aspect to Saturn. Adding to this event is Venus; between January 1 and 10, heliocentric Venus will be at a torque-maximizing 180-degrees opposite to Earth and also to Jupiter. This will be followed by Mercury passing 90-degrees to Saturn and Venus passing 60-degrees to Saturn. Moon will be at its declination minimum on January 16.

From mid-January to around January 23, Mercury will make 180-degree oppositions to Earth and Jupiter as well as a 60-degree aspect to Saturn. The month will finish up with Mercury making a torque-maximizing 0-degree conjunction to Venus. Moon will be at its maximum declination on January 30.

## February 2026

February 3-4 will see Mercury pass 120-degrees to Jupiter and a torque-enhancing 0-degrees to Saturn. Between February 9-11, Mercury will be 90-degrees square to Jupiter and 120-degrees to Earth. In the midst of this, Moon will be at its declination minimum on February 13.

Mercury will then take up a 90-degree square aspect to Earth on February 15-16 followed by a 60-degree aspect to Jupiter. From February 16-20, Venus will pass 120-degrees to Jupiter.

Mercury will be at perihelion on February 19. February 20-22 will see Venus pass 90-degrees to Mercury and 120-degrees to Jupiter. Mercury will pass 60-degress to Earth. On February 23-24, Mercury and Jupiter will be at a torque-enhancing 0-degree conjunction. February 22-25 will see Venus making a 0-degree conjunction to Saturn and a brief 90-degree aspect to Mercury. The month will conclude with Moon at maximum declination on February 26. Venus will be 120-degrees to Mercury on February 27-28.

## March 2026

From March 6-9, Mercury will be conjunct Earth. This event on a geocentric horoscope wheel is what astrologers would call Mercury retrograde. Such events are noted for trend changes and emotional reactions. Traders and investors should be alert to possible trend changes. Mercury will also pass 60-degrees to Jupiter during this event.

From March 9-12, Mercury will be 180-degrees opposite Saturn while Jupiter is 90-degrees square to Venus. On March 12, Moon will be at declination minimum. March 12-18 will see Earth and Jupiter at a 90-degrees square aspect. From March 16-18, Mercury will make a 90-degree aspect to Jupiter. Earth will then take on a torque-generating 180-degree opposition aspect to Saturn which will remain in place until month-end. Moon will pass through zero-degrees declination on March 19 and through maximum declination on March 25.

From March 26-29, Jupiter will be 120-degrees trine Mercury. Venus will be 180-degrees opposite Mercury from March 22 to month end. Saturn will be 120-degrees to Jupiter from March 27 to month end. Mercury will be 120-degrees to Saturn March 29-30.

## April 2026

April starts off with Moon at zero-degrees declination. Mercury will pass 60-degrees to Earth on April 1-3. Venus will be 60-degrees to Saturn at this time also. This will be followed on April 7-8 by Moon at its declination minimum. April 9-11 will see Mercury pass 90-degrees square to Saturn.

Slower moving aspects in April will include Earth at a 120-degree trine to Venus from April 11-23 and Earth 120-degrees to Jupiter from April 11-23.

On April 15, Moon will pass through zero-degrees declination.. From April 15 to 19, Mercury and Jupiter will be at a torque-building 180-degree opposition one another. During this same period, Earth and Mercury will make a 90-degree aspect. Mercury and Saturn will make a brief 60-degree aspect. Venus will be 90-degrees to Saturn April 19-24.

Moon will pass its declination maximum on April 21. This will be followed April 27-30 by Mercury 120-degrees trine to Earth. The month will finish out with Moon at zero-degrees declination on April 28.

## May 2026

May 5 will see Moon at its declination minimum. Jupiter will be 120-degrees trine Mercury May 4-5. Early May will also see Mercury and Saturn will make a 0-degree conjunction. In addition, Venus and Saturn will be at 120-degrees trine May 3-9. From May 5-10 Venus will be at a torque-enhancing 0-degree conjunction to Jupiter. This will be closely followed by Venus at 120-degrees to Saturn and Mercury and Venus making a 90-degree square to one another. On May 13, Moon will pass through zero-degrees declination.

Toward the end of the Venus-Jupiter conjunction, Mercury will be opposite Earth (May 14-16) which will maximize torque on the Sun's surface. Mercury will then pass 60-degrees to Saturn and Jupiter. May 17-25 will see Mercury making a 60-degree aspect to Venus, a 90-degree aspect to Saturn, and Earth making a 120-degree aspect to Saturn. Earth makes a 120-degree aspect to Jupiter as well.

Mercury will be at perihelion on May 18. During this time, Moon will be at its declination maximum on May 19. Saturn will be 120-degrees trine Earth from May 17-25.

From May 25-26, Mercury and Earth will be 120-degrees trine as will Mercury and Saturn. Jupiter will be conjunct Mercury May 24-26. From May 25 to month-end, Earth and Venus will be 90-degrees square. The month will wrap up with Moon at zero-degrees declination on May 25 while Venus and Mercury are at a torque-building conjunction.

## June 2026

June will start off with Moon at its declination minimum. Mercury and Venus will complete their conjunction by June 3. Earth and Venus/Mercury will be 90-degrees square during this time as well. Saturn will be 180-degrees opposite Mercury June 8-9. For most of the month, Jupiter will be 90-degrees square Earth. June 9 will have Moon passing through zero-degrees declination. June 11-12 will see Mercury pass 60-degrees to Earth.

June 14-16 will have Mercury square Jupiter. June 15 will see Moon at its declination maximum. From June 16 to 19, Venus will be 180-degrees opposite Saturn. From June 23 through month end, Earth and Saturn will be at a 90-degree aspect. During this same time, Jupiter will be 120-degrees trine Mercury. The month will conclude with Moon at its declination minimum on June 29.

## July 2026

The first two weeks of July will have Venus 90-degrees square to Jupiter and 60-degrees to Mercury. July 8-14 will have Earth conjunct Mercury. This event on a geocentric horoscope wheel is what astrologers would call Mercury retrograde. Such events are noted for trend changes and emotional reactions. In the midst of this timespan, Moon will be at its declination maximum on July 13. A trend change in this two-week time span is likely.

July 16-19 will have Mercury 180-degrees opposite to Jupiter and also 60-degrees to Saturn. Moon will pass through zero-degrees declination on July 19. Venus will pass 60-degrees to Earth July 14-20. July 20 through month end will have Earth 180-degrees opposite Jupiter. On July 26, Moon will be at its declination minimum. Mercury and Venus will make a 90-degree square July 25-28. Venus will be 120-degrees to Saturn as well.

## August 2026

The month starts with Earth still 180-degrees opposite Jupiter. Jupiter and Saturn are still at 120-degrees to one another. The Earth/Jupiter aspect will fade by August 4 just as Moon is at zero declination. August 1-2 will see Mercury make a conjunction to Saturn. August 1-2 will have Mercury at a 120-degree aspect to Jupiter. This will be followed by Earth 60-degrees to Saturn and Venus 120-degrees to Mercury. Jupiter and Mercury will then pass 90-degrees square August 7-8.

Mercury will then move into a square aspect to Earth on August 8-10. Moon will be at its maximum declination on August 9. August 10 will have Moon at perigee. This could result in a trend change.

August 13-16 will have Venus 90-degrees to Saturn. From August 14-15, Mercury will be 120-degrees trine to Earth. August 15 will have Moon at zero-degrees declination. August 14 will have Mercury at perihelion which could add to market volatility.

Venus will be a torque-sensitive 180-degrees to Mercury on August 18-19. Mercury will also pass 90-degrees to Saturn. August 22 will have Moon at its declination minimum. On either side of this Moon event, Mercury will make a conjunction to Jupiter (August 22-23). Watch for a possible trend change. The month will conclude with Moon at zero-degrees declination and Earth at a 180-degree aspect to Mercury.

## September 2026

The month will start off with Venus at 60-degrees to Saturn. Venus will also be 180-degrees to Jupiter. Moon will be at declination maximum on September 5. This declination event will be bracketed by Mercury making a 180-degree opposition to Saturn on September 4-5.Venus will also be making a 120-degree aspect to Mercury.

Moon will be at zero-degrees declination on September 11. This event will be followed by Mercury making a 90-degree square aspect to Jupiter September 13-15. This will be followed by Mercury at a 120-degree aspect to Earth September 17-21.

September 19 will have Moon at declination minimum. This will be followed by Mercury at a 120-degree aspect to Jupiter September 23-26. Mercury will be 120-degrees to Saturn at this time too. From September 25 through month end, Mercury will be 90-degrees square Venus. Moon will be at zero-degrees declination on September 26.

## October 2026

Moon will be at its declination maximum as the month gets underway.

From October 1-7, Earth will be 0-degrees conjunct Saturn. Earth will be 120-degrees trine Jupiter as well. Mercury will be 90-degrees to Earth October 5-7.

From October 9 through month end, Venus will transit past the Earth/Saturn pairing. This transit could well result in a trend change. The Earth/Saturn conjunction ends on October 11. Venus will pass 120-degrees to Jupiter October 11-13. This will be followed by Mercury making a 180-degree opposition to Jupiter on October 13-17. In addition, Mercury will pass 60-degrees to Venus.

October 16 will have Moon at its declination minimum. October 19-21 will see Mercury 60-degrees to Earth. This will be followed by Venus passing a torque-building 0-degrees to Earth October 19-29. October 23 will have Moon passing through zero-degrees of declination.

As the month ends, Moon will be at declination maximum. As well, from October 28 to month end, Mercury will make a 0-degree conjunction to Saturn. Venus will pass 90-degrees to Jupiter.

## November 2026

The month starts off with a series of events: Mercury conjunct Earth (Mercury retrograde), Mercury conjunct Venus, and Mercury/Venus square Jupiter. These events will enhance the gravitational torque on the Sun. Look for increased market volatility.

On November 5, Moon will pass through zero-degrees declination. November 4-9 will have Earth square Jupiter. November 9-10 will have Mercury pass 60-degrees to Jupiter.

November 12 will have Moon at its declination minimum. November 14-15 will have Mercury at 90-degrees to Saturn. November 18-21 will have Mercury passing Jupiter while Venus makes a 60-degree aspect to Jupiter. November 20 will have Moon passing through zero-degrees of declination. Mercury will make a square to Earth on November 21-22. Venus and Mercury will pass 60-degrees to one another as well. November 26 will have Moon at declination maximum. The month finishes up with Mercury 120-degrees to Earth and Venus 90-degrees to Mercury.

## December 2026

The month starts with Mercury 120-degrees to Earth, Moon at zero-degrees declination, and Mercury opposite Saturn.

December 6-10 will have Saturn 90-degrees square Venus. December 10-11 will have Moon passing through its declination minimum. Mercury will make a 120-degree trine aspect to Venus and a 90-degree aspect to Jupiter during the timeframe December 14-20. December 17 will have Moon passing through zero-degrees declination.

Mercury and Venus will make a 120-degree trines to Jupiter and Saturn on December 23-25. This will be followed closely by Moon at its declination maximum. Mercury will be at perihelion on December 24. December 27-30 will have Venus conjunct Jupiter. The month will finish up with Moon at zero-degrees declination and Mercury 180-degrees to Earth.

# FINAL WORDS

I have taken you on a wide-ranging journey to acquaint you with the connection between heliocentric planetary activity and market price behavior. I sincerely hope you will embrace planetary movements, aspects, and cycles as valuable tools to assist you in your trading and investing activity.

I hope you will pause often to contemplate the price action you see unfolding on stocks, commodities, and indices. Are these ups and downs in price strictly an emotional reaction of market participants to events in the cosmos, or are traders at large investment institutions anticipating planetary events and taking action before individual traders and investors?

If you decide to embrace financial astrology as a tool to help you navigate the markets, I encourage you to stick with it. At first it might seem daunting, but fight the urge to give up. Soon enough, trading and investing will take on a new meaning.

To encourage you, I will leave you with the words of Neil Turok from his 2012 book, *The Universe Within:*

"Perseverance leads to enlightenment. And the truth is more beautiful than your wildest dreams."

# NOTES

Figure 1-1: Loes Ten Kate, I. (2006) *Organics on Mars -Laboratory studies of organic material under simulated Martian conditions.* Ph.D. Thesis.

Figure 1-2: https://www.elsaelsa.com/astrology/zodiac-sign-glyphs.

Bayer, G. (1940). *Stock and Commodity Traders Handbook of Trend Determination*. Self-published, Carmel, California.

Bigg, E.K. (1967). Influence of the Planet Mercury on Sunspots. *Astronomical Journal.* Vol. 72, p. 463.

Cao, J., et al. (2024). Key Questions of Earth-Wind and Moon Interaction. *Space, Science, and Technology.* vol. 4, Article 0094.

Chubykalo, A., Espinoza, A.(2014) The Mathematical Justification of a Possible Wave Nature of the Time Flow of Kozyrev. *International Journal of Physics and Astronomy.* Vol. 2.

Fairbridge, R. W. (1984). Planetary periodicities and terrestrial climate stress. In: *Climatic Changes on a Yearly to Millennial Basis: Geological, Historical and Instrumental Records.* pp: 509-520. Dordrecht: Springer Netherlands.

Gutzwiller, M. (1998). Moon-Earth-Sun: The Oldest Three-Body Problem. *Review of Modern Physics.* vol. 70, p.589.

Hung, C-C. (2007). Apparent Relations Between Solar Activity and solar Tides Caused by Planets. NASA/TM 2007-14817.

Jelbring, H. (2013). Energy transfer in the solar system. *Pattern Recognition in Physics.* vol 1, pp:165–176.

Jelbring, H. (2013). Celestial commensurabilities: some special cases. Pattern Recognition in Physics. vol 1, pp: 143–146.

King, J.W., Willis, D.M. (1974). Magnetometeorology: Relationships Between the Weather and Earth's Magnetic Field. NASA. Goddard Space Flight Center.

Kozyrev, N.A. (1971). On the possibility of experimental investigation of the properties of time. In: *Time in Science and Philosophy.* pp. 111-132. Prague.

Krausz, R. (1998). The New Gann Swing Chartist. *Stocks & Commodities.* vol 16, no. 2, pp: 57-66.

McWhirter, L. (1938). *McWhirter Theory of Stock Market Forecasting.* Astro Book Company, USA.

Mörner, N-A. (2013). *Planetary influence on the Sun and the Earth, and a Modern Book-Burning.* pp. 39-50.

Mörner, N.-A., et al. (2013). General conclusions regarding the planetary–solar–terrestrial interaction. *Pattern Recognition in Physics,* vol. 1, pp: 205–206.

Mörner, N.-A., Tattersall, R., & Solheim, J.-E. (2013). Preface: Pattern in solar variability, their planetary origin and terrestrial impacts. *Pattern Recognition in Physics,* vol 1, pp: 203–204.

Nordling, C., Osterman, J. (1980). *Physics Handbook,* Student Literatur, Lund, Sweden.

Read, B. (1970). Fibonacci Series in the Solar System. *The Fibonacci Quarterly.* October issue, p. 428.

Scafetta, N., Bianchini, A. (2022). The Planetary Theory of Solar Variability: A Review. *Frontiers in Astronomy and Space Science.* vol. 9. pp:1-28.

Scafetta, N. (2014). The Complex Planetary Synchronization Structure of the Solar System. *Pattern Recognition in Physics.* vol. 2, pp:1-19.

Schade, G. (2022.) The Origins Of The Stochastic Oscillator. *CMT Association Journal.*

Seddon, C. (2021). *Mercury: Elusive Messenger of the Gods.* Glanville Press, USA.

Sherrard, M. et al (2018). Low intensity electromagnetic fields induce human cryptochromes to moderate intracellular reactive oxygen species. *PLoS Biology.* vol. 16, no. 10.

Shikhobalov, L. S. (1996). The fundamentals of N. A. Kozyrev's Causal Mechanics In: *On the Way to Understanding the Time*

*Phenomenon: The Constructions of Time in Natural Science.* World Scientific. Singapore.

Tattersall, R. (2013). The Hum: log-normal distribution and planetary-solar resonance. *Pattern Recognition in Physics.* vol. 1, pp:185-198.

Turok, N. (2012). *The Universe Within.* House of Anansi Press, Canada.

Wilson, I.R.G. (2013). The Venus-Earth-Jupiter pin-Orbit Coupling Model. *Pattern Recognition in Physics.* vol. 1, pp:147-158.

Wolff, C.L., Patrone, P.N. (2010). A New Way That Planets Can Affect the Sun. *Solar Physics.* vol. 266, pp: 227-246.

Youseff, M. (2016). Hyperkalemia, the sodium potassium model and the heart. *E-Journal of Cardiology Practice.* vol 14. No. 11.

# GLOSSARY

**Anomalistic Month:** An anomalistic month is the time of takes Moon to go from being at perigee (closest to Earth) to once again being at perigee, about 27.5 days.

**Ascendant:** one of four cardinal points on a horoscope, the Ascendant denotes the constellation visible at a given time on the eastern horizon.

**Aspect:** the angular relationship between two planets measured in degrees.

**Autumnal Equinox (see Equinox):** the time of year when Sun is at zero-degrees Libra.

**Carrington Cycle:** In 1859, British astronomer Richard Carrington observed that the part of the Sun at 26-degrees above its equatorial mid-point where mass coronal ejections originate had an axial spin rate of 25.38 days – the Carrington Cycle.

**Celestial Equator:** the projection into space of the Earth's equator.

**Conjunct:** an angular relationship of zero-degrees between two planets.

**Declination:** the amount (in degrees) that a planet wanders above or below the ecliptic plane as measured using heliocentric data.

**Draconitic Month:** A draconitic month is the time for the Moon to go from being conjunct the North Node of Moon to once again being conjunct the North Node. On average, this timeframe is 27.2 days.

**Ecliptic Plane:** the plane of motion traveled by the planets as they orbit the Sun.

**Electron Transport Chain:** electrons from a cell's inner mitochondrial membrane contact proteins to create ATP cellular energy.

**Ephemeris:** a daily tabular compilation of planetary and lunar positions.

**Equinox:** an event occurring twice annually that marks the time when the tilt of the Earth's axis is neither toward nor away from the Sun.

**Fibonacci Sequence:** a recursive mathematical sequence in which a given term is the sum of the two preceding terms. (The infinite sequence is as follows: 0,1,1,2,3,5,8,13,21,34,55,89…).

**Gann Master Cycle:** the 19.86-year time span from heliocentric Saturn and Jupiter being conjunct to once again being conjunct.

**Geocentric:** planetary location system in which the vantage point for determining planetary aspects is the Earth.

**Geometric Mean:** the square root of the product of two values.

**Heliocentric:** planetary location system in which the vantage point for determining planetary aspects is the Sun.

**Horoscope:** an image of the zodiac overlaid with the positions of the planets.

**Inferior Conjunction:** on a geocentric zodiac wheel, an inferior conjunction occurs when retrograde Mercury or Venus is 0-degrees conjunct the Sun. On the heliocentric zodiac wheel, the inferior conjunction will have these planets 0-degrees conjunct to Earth.

**Kozyrev:** Nikolai Kozyrev was a little-known 1950s era Russian astrophysicist who advanced the idea was that space-time itself is a source of torsional (torque) energy. This energy is intensified at various times due to the spatial heliocentric geometries (aspects) of the planets.

**Latitude:** the position of a planet above or below the Earth's equator line.

**Lunar Month:** (see Synodic Month).

**McWhirter Cycle:** The 18.6-year time span in which the North Node progresses around the 12 zodiac signs.

**North Node of Moon:** the intersection points between the Moon's plane and Earth's ecliptic are termed the *North* and *South* nodes (Astrologers tend to focus on the North node and Ephemeris tables list the zodiacal position of the North Node for each calendar day.)

**Periodogram:** a method using Fourier mathematics to identify dominant frequencies and recurring patterns in data.

**Retrograde motion:** the apparent backwards motion of a planet through the zodiac signs when viewed from a vantage point on Earth.

**ROS (reactive Oxygen species):** formed in human cells as a result of a redox reaction malfunction in the electron transport chain.

**Sidereal Month:** the Moon orbits Earth with a slightly elliptical pattern in approximately 27.3 days, relative to a fixed frame of reference.

**Sidereal Orbital Period:** the time required for a planet to make one full orbit of the Sun as viewed from a fixed vantage point on the Sun.

**Sodium Potassium Model:** brain cells have concentration gradients of sodium ions ($Na^+$) outside the cell walls and concentration gradients of potassium ions ($K^+$) inside the cell walls. A stimulus event, such as an increase in electromagnetic particles hitting the human body, will cause a cellular reaction in which ion channels open and $Na^+$ ions move out of the cells and $K^+$ ions move into the cells.

**Solstice:** occurring twice annually, a solstice event marks the time when the Sun reaches its highest or lowest altitude above the horizon at noon.

**Superior Conjunction:** on a geocentric zodiac wheel, superior conjunction occurs when retrograde Mercury or Venus is 0-degrees conjunct the Sun. On the heliocentric zodiac wheel, the superior conjunction will have these planets 180-degrees opposite to Earth.

**Synodic Month:** from a moving frame of reference, the 29.5-day time span for the Moon to orbit the Earth.

**Synodic Orbital Period:** the time required for a planet to make one full orbit of the Sun as viewed from a fixed vantage point on Earth.

**Transiting:** the action of a planet moving past a selected point of the zodiac wheel.

**Vernal Equinox:** the time of the year when Sun is at zero-degrees Aries.

**Zodiac:** an imaginary band encircling the 360-degrees of the planetary system divided into twelve equal portions of 30-degrees each.

**Zodiac Wheel:** a circular image broken into 12 portions of 30-degrees each. Each portion represents a different astrological sign.

# APPENDIX 1

# The Trend

The concept of price trend is not new. Traders on Wall Street were using trend changes as a strategy already in the 1930s. Today, however, market analysts and commentators seldom refer to the trend of a stock or commodity. Traders and investors should not think the trend is no longer important. It is vitally important to surviving in today's volatile markets. When studying the price movement of stocks, indices, and commodity futures, one will *often* find that the price trend changes at planetary events. To confirm that the planetary event is in fact causing a trend change, how then does one determine that the trend is changing?

## *Trend Changes According to W.D. Gann*

W.D. Gann focused on the *swing point* as his way of determining changes in the trend. He defined the swing point as the price bar where the *direction of travel* changes.

Gann's *Prior Peak* rule says to watch for times after seeing a swing point when price surpasses the prior swing point. In Figure A-1, a swing point has been labeled in January 2025 on a daily chart of Joby Aviation (JOBY).

A trader seeking to take a long position in JOBY would buy if and only if the price of the stock surpassed the prior peak at $10.72. A buy signal was created in July 2025 when price surpassed the swing point of $10.72. The stock went on to rally to near $21 per share.

**Figure A-1**
Joby Aviation (JOBY)

Commodity futures are notoriously more volatile than most stocks. To better manage trading risk, W.D. Gann advised to examine a weekly price chart. Figure A-2 illustrates Soybean futures price action in weekly chart format.

**Figure A-2**
Soybean futures (weekly)

The chart has been overlaid with a dashed line starting from a $10.69 swing point in September 2024. From September 2024 through to late October 2025, Soybeans failed to close on a weekly basis above this price level. Finally, in late October a buying opportunity surfaced when price surpassed $10.69.

## The Trend According to Harold Gartley

Harold Gartley was born in New Jersey in 1899. When he was 12 years old, he got a summer job on the floor of the New York Stock Exchange as an odd-lot runner. It was his job to literally run around the NYSE trading floor looking for buyers and sellers of odd-lots of shares needed to fill orders. For example, if the brokerage firm Gartley worked for received an order to buy 210 shares of ABC Company, the even-lot, 200-share part of the order would easily be filled. It was then young Harold's job to find a trader on the NYSE floor who wanted to sell him the 10 shares of ABC stock to complete the 210-share odd-lot order.

He was so enamored with the operation of the NYSE he decided to carve out a successful career as a trader and financial advisor. To realize this goal, he attended New York University where he received his Bachelor's Degree in Commercial Science followed by a Master's Degree in Business Administration. In 1936, he created a home-study course entitled *Profits in the Stock Market.* This course material established Harold Gartley as an authority on the subject of market trends.

### *Major Trend*

Gartley focused on two trends: the *major* and the *intermediate*. In his home-study course, Gartley defined the major trend as being relative to the 200-day moving average. Times when price action is above the 200-day average represents a bullish major trend. Times when price action is below the 200-day average represents a bearish major trend.

Figure A-3 illustrates a daily chart of fin-tech banking operator Sofi Technologies (SOFI). The chart has been overlaid with the 200-day moving average. The stock broke above its 200-day average in April 2025. The bullish trend has remained in place since.

**Figure A-3**
SOFI with 200-day average

## *Intermediate Trend*

In the early 1900s, Charles Dow (after whom the Dow Jones Average is partly named) observed that within a bull market or a bear market, there will be times when prices move counter to the bull or bear trend. These movements comprised of see-saw price action are what Gartley termed *intermediate trends.* Gartley suggested that after an intermediate movement in one direction, it is common to observe a corrective movement of 33 to 66% in the opposite direction, thus creating the see-saw pattern on the price chart. What Gartley was likely alluding to with his 33 to 66% observation is Fibonacci retracements (38.2% and 61.8%).

Gartley referred to the see-saw patterns on a price chart as *cycles*. He concluded that each cycle will have two components: a component that moves in the same direction as the prevailing major trend and a corrective component that moves counter to the direction of the major trend. Gartley said that an intermediate bullish trend comprises cycles that go from a price low to a subsequent price low. An intermediate bearish trend comprises cycles that go from a price high to a subsequent price high.

Gartley advised to draw a line that connects the sequential low points in a rising price scenario and a line that roughly connects the sequential high points in a rising price scenario. The resulting lines he called the *intermediate trend lines.*

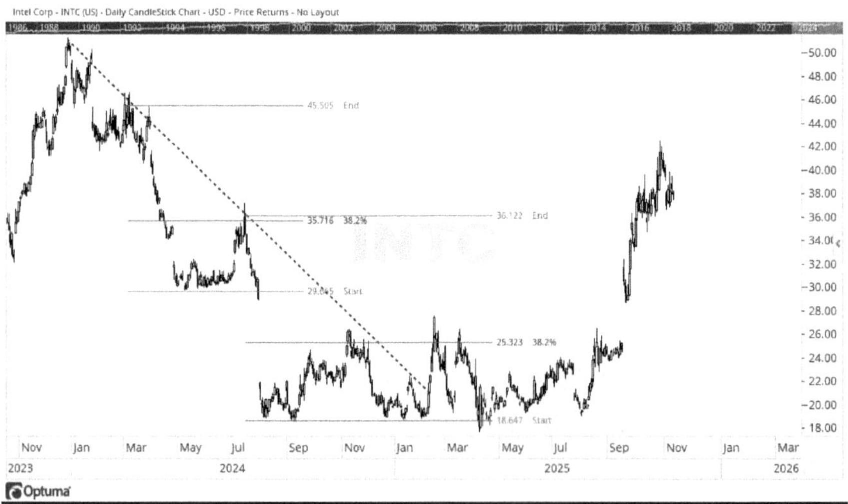


**Figure A-4**
Intel (INTC) with Gartley trends

To illustrate, consider the chart in Figure A-4 of chipmaker Intel (INTC). From a high in January 2024, price began to decline. Subsequent rally attempts all failed to take out the intermediate downtrend line. The move lower from March to May 2024 was met with a rally attempt that turned out to be a Fibonacci 38.2 % value just as Gartley suggested. The steep drop from July to September 2024 was met with another Fibonacci 38.2% retrace effort which too failed to take out the intermediate trend line. Finally in mid-February 2025, price was able to break above the trend line and a buy signal was created.

## Oscillator Functions

Trend can also be determined using a mathematical construct called an *oscillator*. Consider price data from a moving period of n=14 days. On day n=15, the price can be expressed as a percentage of the highest price observed over the past n=14 days. On day n=16, the price can be expressed as a percentage of the highest price observed over the past n=14 days. If this percentage value is seen to be rising as subsequent prices are examined, price momentum (the trend) is deemed to be bullish. As this calculated percentage value begins to slow, an alert trader will start to anticipate a possible bearish price trend manifesting.

A plot of these percentage values on a chart with a vertical scale of 0 to 100 is termed an oscillator. If the price data input into the oscillator function calculations is random, the oscillator is termed a *stochastic oscillator.* Price data of stocks, commodity futures, ETFs, and indices are *random signals.* That is, the price on a given day is not a guaranteed reflection of price the day before or the day after.

Oscillators were first applied to stock market data in the late 1940s. Back then, price data had to be read from a ticker tape, and then processed with a pencil, paper, and slide rule. Today, oscillator functions can be applied with the click of a computer mouse and software functions.

## Fast Stochastic Oscillator

The *Fast Stochastic Oscillator* was derived in 1948 by Chicago-based stock and commodity trader Ralph Dystant. Mr. Dystant also operated a trading school called *Investment Educators.* A staff member at the school in the 1950s was George Lane who would go on to enjoy a stellar career as a chartist and trader.

The Fast Stochastic Oscillator is based on both the lowest price and highest price over a recent span of *n* price bars on a chart. The closing price on a given day relative to these reference points creates an output value called %K, calculated as:

$$\%K = 100 * [(\text{Closing price} - Ln)/(Hn - Ln)] ;$$

where Ln is the lowest price in the past *n* periods, Hn is the highest price in the past n periods, and Closing Price is the close of the current day's trading session.

The Fast Stochastic also comprises a value called %D which is calculated as follows:

$$\%D = 100 * [(\text{Closing price} - L3)/(H3 - L3)] ;$$

where L3 is the lowest price in the past 3 periods, H3 is the highest price in the past 3 periods, and Closing Price is the close of the current day's trading session. In most software programs, the pre-configured settings for the Fast Stochastic are n=10 price bars and 3 periods for the %D calculation.

Dystant and his team said that a Fast Stochastic value of 20 is generally representative of a stock, commodity or index that is oversold and ready for a turn bullish. They regarded a value of 80 to be overbought and ready to turn bearish.

To illustrate, the chart of artificial intelligence company Leidos Holdings (LDOS) in Figure A-5 has been fitted with the Fast Stochastic in the lower pane. Market action today is more volatile than in the 1950s. This makes the Fast Stochastic somewhat challenging to use in that frequent buy or sell signals might be encountered. The chart has further been fitted with arrows at the various buy and sell signals.

**Figure A-5**
Leidos Holdings (N: LDOS) with Fast Stochastic

## Slow Stochastic

In the mid-1950s, George Lane created the *Slow Stochastic* as a simplified variation of the Fast Stochastic. In the Slow Stochastic, the %D is taken as being a 3-bar simple moving average of the %K function. This results in the profile of the Slow Stochastic plot being smoother than that of the Fast Stochastic.

Figure A-6 illustrates a daily price chart of cruise boat operator Carnival Corporation (CCL). The lower pane of the chart illustrates the Slow Stochastic using 21 price bars and a 5-bar %D. This setting happens to be the personal preference of this author.

**Figure A-6**
Carnival Corp. (CCL) with Slow Stochastic

At the far left of the chart, a buy signal is generated when the Stochastic gets above its upper boundary line. The ensuing rally lasts until mid-December, 2024 when the Stochastic falls beneath its upper boundary. Another buy signal is generated in mid-January 2025 when the Stochastic bounces off its lower boundary. Herein is a challenge with the Slow Stochastic; frequent buy signals might be generated. The ensuing rally was a short one and faltered in early February. The stock then declined until mid-April 2025. The Gartley method shows a downward dashed line which reflects a bearish trend. As price moved above the Gartley trend line, the Stochastic delivered a bullish crossover. A trader could have bought at this crossover, or waited until the Stochastic moved above the upper boundary line. Price action faltered a bit in June and the Stochastic faded below the upper boundary. However, this proved to be a false signal (a potential weakness of the Slow Stochastic). A trader could have re-entered the trade using the Gann Prior Peak method. In late July, the Stochastic again faded below the upper boundary as the stock lapsed into a sideways consolidation. In late August, the Gann Prior Peak method intersected with a Stochastic crossover. However, an alert trader would have noticed that price at this point had moved a 1.382 X multiple of the January to April decline. And true to form, the Stochastic promptly rolled over to give a sell signal. Gains on this trade would have been miniscule.

## MAC-D

In 1979, technical chartist Gerald Appel considered the relation between two exponential moving averages (EMA) of price data. He focused on 26 and 12-period exponential averages of closing prices (n=26 and n=12). He deemed the 26-period average to be slow moving versus the faster 12-period average. He wrote a computer algorithm to calculate and plot the difference value between the two exponential averages. He called this difference value the *indicator line.* His algorithm then calculated a 9-period exponential moving average of the indicator line values and plotted them to create the *signal line.*

Gerald Appel's indicator is now formally known as the *Moving Average Convergence Divergence* indicator and is abbreviated *MAC-D.* The MAC-D formula is as follows:

MAC-D = [(12 day EMA – 26 day EMA)].

Crossovers of the indicator line above or below the signal line can be used to gauge changes in price trend. Moves of the MAC-D line above or below the zero line of the output plot can also be used to discern trend changes.

The chart in Figure A-7 illustrates price action of The Metals Company (ticker symbol TMC) who are setting up to engage in sub-sea mining in the South Pacific.

**Figure A-7**
The Metals Corp (TMC) with MAC-D

Between April and June 2025, the MAC-D gave a number of crossover signals as the stock moved higher. This is a potential weakness of the MAC-D. Share price peaked in late June, but the MAC-D still had not recorded a crossover. In late August, a crossover signal was generated and price rallied to near $11. As price peaked, the MAC-D had not yet delivered a crossover warning.

## True Strength Index

**Figure A-8**
The Metals Corp (TMC) with True Strength Index

The True Strength Index was developed by mathematician and trader William Blau in the 1990s. It is a double-smoothed indicator. The close between the present day and the previous day help to define momentum. An exponential moving average of n=25 momentum values is calculated. An exponential moving average of n=13 of these exponential values is next calculated. The final component of the indicator is an exponential average of the indicator itself. This is called the Signal Line and is usually taken as n=7 periods.

Figure A-8 illustrates price action of TMC with the True Strength Indicator (TSI) applied. The TSI avoids many of the weaknesses of other oscillator-type indicators.

# ABOUT THE AUTHOR

Malcolm Bucholtz, B.Sc, MBA, M.Sc., is a graduate of Queen's University (Faculty of Engineering) in Canada and Heriot Watt University in Scotland (where he received an MBA degree and a M.Sc. degree). After working in Canadian industry for far too many years, Malcolm followed his passion for the financial markets by becoming an Investment Advisor/Commodity Trading Advisor with an independent brokerage firm in western Canada. Today, he resides in Saskatchewan, Canada where he trades the financial markets using technical chart analysis, esoteric mathematics, and the planetary principles outlined in this book.

Malcolm is the author of several books. His first book, T*he Bull, the Bear and the Planets,* offers the reader an introduction to financial astrology and makes the case that there are esoteric and astrological phenomena that influence the financial markets. His second book, *The Lost Science*, takes the reader on a deeper journey into planetary events and unique mathematical phenomena that influence financial markets. His third book, *De-Mystifying the McWhirter Theory of Stock Market Forecasting* seeks to simplify and illustrate the McWhirter methodology. *The Cosmic Clock* follows from the *Lost Science* and helps the reader become better acquainted with planetary events that influence markets. Malcolm has been writing the *Financial Astrology Almanac* each year since 2014. In 2023, he also released *Follow the Trend,* a book to assist traders and investors in identifying price trend changes on indices, stocks, and commodity futures.

Malcolm maintains a website (www.investingsuccess.ca) where he provides traders and investors with astrological insights into the financial markets. He also offers the *Astrology Letter* and the *Cycle Report* in which subscribers receive twice-monthly previews of pending astrological events that stand to influence markets.

# OTHER BOOKS BY THE AUTHOR

## Follow The Trend

Geopolitical unrest, increasing inflation and interest rates, financial blogs and media channels with rock-star status fund managers touting the latest, greatest investment idea. The emotions of traders and investors are continually being pulled in multiple directions at once. What to buy? When to buy? When to sell? At times the noise can be deafening.

This book introduces the reader to the concept of the *trend*; the direction of price movement. Is price moving in a bullish direction or bearish direction? Is the trend changing? Paying attention to changes of trend on a stock, an index, an ETF, or a commodity futures contract can help traders and investors tune out the noise and re-gain a sense of clarity.

The trend is seldom mentioned in financial media. Instead, the media serves up a constant stream of angst and drama. The trend is also ignored by individual financial advisors who prefer to promote the strategy of buying and holding for the long term. This book pushes back against the angst, drama, and passive complacency that pervades our investment decision making. There was a time when the trend *was* followed. In the 1930s, H.M. Gartley taught investors how to use major and intermediate trend lines to make better buying and selling decisions. W.D. Gann also focused on the trend, using swing points to delineate buying and selling opportunities. The 1980s and 1990s heralded computer algorithms and chart technical indicators to more effectively demarcate changes in trend.

*Follow The Trend* shows the reader how to apply trend lines and swing points to make buy and sell decisions. This book goes on to examine a number of chart technical indicators and answers the following questions: How are they mathematically structured? What do they reveal about the trend? How should they be interpreted? Are some better than others? Follow The Trend – When to Buy and When to Sell offers a fresh way to look at trading and investing, giving the reader the knowledge to answer the two critical questions: When to Buy? When to Sell?

## The Cosmic Clock

Are price swings on Crude Oil, Soybeans, the British pound and other financial instruments a reflection of planetary placements?

Can the movements of the Moon affect the stock market?

The answer to these questions is YES. Changes in price trends on the markets are in fact related to our changing emotions. Our emotions, in turn, are impacted by the changing events in our cosmos.

In the early part of the 20th century, many successful traders on Wall Street, including the venerable W.D. Gann and the mysterious Louise McWhirter, understood that emotion was linked to the forces of the cosmos. They used geocentric astrological events and esoteric mathematics to predict changes in price trend and to profit from the markets.

However, by the latter part of the 20th century, the investment community had become more comfortable in relying on academic financial theory and the opinions of colorful television media personalities, all wrapped up in a buy and hold mentality.

*The Cosmic Clock* has been written for traders and investors who are seeking to gain an introductory understanding of the cosmic forces that influence emotion and the financial markets.

This book will acquaint you with an extensive range of astrological and mathematical phenomena-from the Golden Mean and Fibonacci Sequence through planetary transit lines, quantum lines, the McWhirter method, planetary conjunctions and market cycles. The numerous illustrated examples show how these unique phenomena can deepen your understanding of the financial markets with the goal of making you a better trader and investor.

## Stock Market Forecasting: The McWhirter Method De-Mystified

Very little is known about Louise McWhirter, except that in 1937 she wrote the book, *McWhirter Theory of Stock Market Forecasting.*

In my travels to places as far away as the British Library in London, England to research financial Astrology, not once did I come across any other books by McWhirter. Nor did I find any other book from her era that even mentioned her name. I find all of this to be deeply mysterious. Whoever she was, she wrote only one book. It is a powerful one that is as accurate today as it was back in 1937. The purpose of writing this book is suggested by the title itself – to de-mystify McWhirter's methodology.

## The Lost Science

The financial markets are a reflection of the psychological emotions of traders and investors. These emotions ebb and flow in harmony with the forces of nature.

Scientific techniques and phenomena such as square root mathematics, the Golden Mean, the Golden Sequence, lunar events, planetary transits and geocentric planetary aspects have been used by civilizations dating as far back as the ancient Egyptians in order to comprehend the forces of nature.

The emotions of traders and investors can fluctuate in accordance with these forces of nature. Lunar events can be seen to align with trend changes on financial markets. Significant market cycles align with planetary transits and aspects. Price patterns on stocks, commodity futures and market indices can be seen to conform to square root and Golden Mean mathematics.

In the early years of the 20th century, the most successful traders on Wall Street, including the venerable W.D. Gann, used these scientific techniques and phenomena to profit from the markets. However, over the ensuing decades as technology has advanced, the science has been lost.

*The Lost Science* acquaints the reader with an extensive range of astrological and mathematical phenomena. From the Golden Mean and Fibonacci Sequence, to planetary transit lines and square roots through to an examination of lunar and planetary aspects, the numerous illustrated examples in this book show the reader how these unique scientific phenomena impact the financial markets.

## The Bull, The Bear and The Planets

Once maligned by many, the subject of financial astrology is now experiencing a revival as traders and investors seek deeper insight into the forces that move the financial markets.

The markets are a dynamic entity fueled by many factors, some of which we can easily comprehend, some of which are esoteric. *The Bull, The Bear and the Planets* introduces the reader to the notion that geocentric astrological phenomena can influence price action on financial markets and create trend changes across both short and longer term time horizons. From an introduction to the historical basics behind astrology through to an examination of lunar astrology and geocentric planetary aspects, the numerous examples in this book will introduce the reader to the power of astrology and its impact on both equity markets and commodity futures markets.

www.ingramcontent.com/pod-product-compliance
Lightning Source LLC
Chambersburg PA
CBHW071206210326
41597CB00016B/1699

* 9 7 8 1 9 9 7 8 6 0 0 4 4 *